Proust's *Recherche*
A Psychoanalytic Interpretation

Randolph Splitter
Professor of English
California Institute of Technology

Proust's *Recherche*
A Psychoanalytic Interpretation

Routledge & Kegan Paul
Boston, London and Henley

First published in 1981
by Routledge & Kegan Paul Ltd
9 Park Street, Boston, Mass. 02108, USA,
39 Store Street, London WC1E 7DD and
Broadway House, Newtown Road,
Henley-on-Thames, Oxon RG 1EN
Set in 10/12 Baskerville by
Saildean Ltd, Surrey
and printed in the United States of America by
Vail-Ballou Press Inc.

British Library Cataloguing in Publication Data

Splitter, Randolph
Proust's 'Recherche'.
1. Proust, Marcel. A la recherche du temps perdu
2. Psychoanalysis and literature
I. Title
843'.912   PQ2631.R63A/   80-41272

ISBN 0 7100 0664 0

For Merle, Jenny, and Jocelyn

Contents

Acknowledgments

For early education and encouragement in the psychoanalytic study of literature, I would like to thank Professor Frederick Crews of the University of California, Berkeley. Our later disagreements over the methods of literary interpretation should not obscure the debt of gratitude I owe him. I would also like to thank my friends and colleagues in the Psychology (otherwise known as Interpretive Studies) Group in the Humanities Division at Caltech for their advice, criticism, and support. I wish to express my appreciation, too, to those who read earlier versions of this study (or related work), for their criticism and (in some cases in particular) their much-needed encouragement: in addition to Professor Crews, Professor Peter Manning of the University of Southern California, Professor Meredith Skura of Rice University, and Professor Joseph Riddel of the University of California at Los Angeles. Indeed, although it is not normally done, I wish to thank the anonymous literary and psychoanalytic readers of Routledge & Kegan Paul, for their sympathetic reading of the manuscript, as well as my gracious and supportive editor Stephen Brook.

I am grateful, also, for the generous research support provided by the Caltech Division of Humanities and Social Sciences and for the generous assistance provided by Valera Hall, Mary Ellis Arnett, and Barbara Calli, who typed various drafts and revisions of the manuscript as if it were some epic work of the order of *A la Recherche* itself. I would like to thank the editors of the following journals, in which earlier versions of portions of this work first appeared: *Literature and Psychology, Hartford Studies in Literature,* and *American Imago.* My deepest debt of gratitude is due, finally, to my wife Merle Splitter, from whom I have learned – about the relations between art and life, between selves and other selves – much that contributed to this study.

. . . le pauvre parricide n'était pas une brute criminelle, un être en dehors de l'humanité, mais un noble exemplaire d'humanité, un homme d'esprit éclairé, un fils tendre et pieux, que la plus inéluctable fatalité . . . a jeté . . . dans un crime et une expiation dignes de demeurer illustres.

Au fond, nous vieillissons, nous tuons tout ce qui nous aime par les soucis que nous lui donnons. . . .

Depuis la mort de mes parents je suis (dans un sens qu'il serait hors de propos de préciser ici) moins moi-même, davantage leur fils.

— Proust, 'Sentiments filiaux d'un parricide'

1 Marcel in Wonderland, or the logic of magical thinking

In two early essays, 'The Sorcerer and his Magic' and 'The Effectiveness of Symbols,' the anthropologist Lévi-Strauss discusses the effectiveness of magical cures.[1] In Proust's 'Combray,' Marcel, suffering from a variety of vague complaints and half-imaginary fears, a chronic state of anxiety, might seem to be a perfect candidate for such 'imaginary' cures. Indeed, both his fears and his deepest wishes reflect primitive, magical, animistic ways of thinking, an uncertainty about the distinction between inner and outer worlds, between animate creatures and inanimate things. In Marcel's eyes the cook Françoise is a primitive who, though she slaughters chickens with sadistic delight, possesses a strict and minute code of behavior, full of irrational prohibitions and an exaggerated faith in the sacred character of dinners. But Marcel treats his mother's goodnight kiss, like Françoise her dinners, as a sacred ceremonial, a nightly ritual betraying compulsive needs over which – so that they don't get out of hand – he must exercise obsessive control. Freud shows how such private ceremonials resemble religious or superstitious practices, particularly in their original forms,[2] and Marcel's aunt Léonie· illustrates the convergence of religion and obsession. As even Piaget's studies of children's thought processes suggest, Marcel's 'primitive' way of seeing things is typically childlike, comparable to the lively imagination of Lewis Carroll's Alice. But his childhood insecurities, his anxieties about inner/outer divisions, and his 'magical' strategies reveal basic structural patterns which are repeated later on every 'level' of the *Recherche*. Lévi-Strauss's essay on 'The Effectiveness of Symbols' describes a shaman helping a woman through a difficult childbirth: in order to become an artist, Marcel, who finally imagines himself as a mother giving birth to art, must also be a shaman, not simply the victim of an imaginary illness but the bearer of a magical cure.

The experience of going to sleep, in the opening pages of the *Recherche,* is one of disorientation, uncertainty, and anxiety.[3] The reader too is disoriented: the first person narrator who starts to tell us all about his nocturnal life is a disembodied presence, a voice speaking to us out of a darkened bedroom. We don't know whether he is young or old but the defenseless, uncertain condition of sleep makes him feel like a child: 'Ou bien en dormant j'avais rejoint sans effort un âge à jamais révolu de ma vie primitive' (I, 4). He experiences again 'childish terrors' like having his curls pulled, as if he were still at the mercy of powerful adults like the great-uncle who pulled the curls. The invalid in the strange hotel who mistakes the light of a gaslamp for the light of a new day is like a child afraid of the dark: 'C'est minuit; on vient d'éteindre le gaz; le dernier domestique est parti et il faudra rester toute la nuit à souffrir sans remède' (I ,4). And this childlike invalid is, we suspect, the narrator himself.

The feeling of being lost, in the dark, makes the narrator lose his sense of identity and doubt his own existence: 'comme j'ignorais où je me trouvais, je ne savais même pas au premier instant qui j'étais' (I, 5). The threat which sleep seems to pose is simply annihilation, death, a fall into the emptiness of *néant.* In the new and unfamiliar room at Balbec (described here first) he will long for death (I, 667), and the objects of that room seem like conscious, malevolent, almost human enemies: hostile curtains, an insolent clock that chatters on as if he were not there, a pitiless mirror with feet (I, 8). This is the animistic world, if not of paranoid delusion, then of childhood, of *Alice in Wonderland,* where there is no clear division between fantasies and reality and where one's private fears may be projected onto the world at large. As in *Alice,* the most threatening aspect of the situation is the size of the room itself, the terror of its high ceiling. Not only do the walls of a room dizzyingly 'tourbillonnaient dans les ténèbres' (I,6), but the narrator's mind ('ma pensée') feels compelled to project itself literally into the room and fill the frightening emptiness created by the high ceiling, 'de se disloquer, de s'étirer en hauteur pour prendre exactement la forme de la chambre et arriver à remplir jusqu'en haut son gigantesque entonnoir' (I, 8). The monstrous funnel seems like the abyss of *néant* turned upside down, in which one may be sucked up and lost forever. It is precisely the emptiness of the high-ceilinged room, its quality of not-being, that most frightens the narrator, and it is this void which he must fill with his own presence, with his own conscious awareness.

Some rooms the narrator remembers fondly, and he likes to make his bed into a nest where he can bury his head and shut himself off from the threatening outer world. He even calls the darkness 'douce et reposante' (I, 3). But, although sleep may be a refuge, bedrooms can be fearful places. Night (in which one loses confidence in visible reality) is a disturbing time, and the fear of darkness, nothingness, and death may also be the fear of losing consciousness in sleep. The experience of going to sleep implies for the narrator a sense of childlike helplessness in the face of overwhelming, even super-natural, forces. And yet this anxiety-filled loss of ordinary conscious control – restored by the reassuring process of what the narrator calls custom or habit (l'habitude')[4] – is also the precondition for a deeper, more valuable, and more gratifying sense of reality. Proust's hero, gazing up at that lofty ceiling like a man with a fear of heights, is like Wordsworth gazing out from the 'awful and sublime' prospect of Mt Snowdon: in both cases the threat of losing oneself in an abyss of nothingness will be overcome by the power of imagination to make all things seem a part of oneself.

The magic lantern of Marcel's Combray childhood – for we learn that the narrator does have a childhood and an identity of his own – though it substitutes light for darkness, disturbs him because it changes the lighting of his bedroom and makes it seem a new, strange, and alien place. The narrator admits that he enjoyed the moving pictures of the magic lantern but insists upon the malaise he felt at

> cette intrusion du mystère et de la beauté dans une chambre que j'avais fini par remplir de mon moi au point de ne pas faire plus attention à elle qu'à lui-même. L'influence anesthésiante de l'habitude ayant cessé, je me mettais à penser, à sentir, choses si tristes' (I, 10).

The comforting sense of shared identity that Marcel feels with his room is also anaesthetic, deadening, and the new elements (mystery and beauty) which undermine the anaesthetic effect create what seems to be a peculiarly pleasurable form of anxiety – the first stage of an aesthetic, rather than anaesthetic, response. Marcel is a cautious, fearful, conservative child; anything new frightens him. He would prefer to live in a hermetically sealed, entirely self-contained world all his own, but the fear of being left open to outside intrusion may give way to the pleasure of incorporating the disturbing element into himself, of restoring the sense that the world is just his private domain. Significantly, the magic lantern by virtue of the magical immateriality of light, performs just this kind of 'transubstantiation' ('transvertébration'):

> Le corps de Golo lui-même, d'une essence aussi surnaturelle que celui de sa monture, s'arrangeait de tout obstacle matériel, de tout objet gênant qu'il rencontrait en le prenant comme ossature et en se le rendant intérieur' (I, 10).

The apparent ability of the magic lantern to assimilate all material objects into itself, though it upsets Marcel's confidence in his surroundings, is actually a visual property which Marcel, implicitly, would like to appropriate for himself.

The scenario of the famous goodnight kiss puts Marcel's anxieties, specifically his anxiety about going to bed, into more personal, social terms. His mother's kiss is a 'communion' (I, 13) by which he can assimilate into himself a magical, immaterial, almost supernatural substance – thereby fulfilling, in a different way, the transmutation that the magic lantern effects – possessing a 'vertu volatile' (I, 23), which turns out to be, simply, the sense of his mother's 'présence' (I, 13). In this way even the material barrier (different bodies) which separates one person from another may be overcome. In short, the kiss is a literally oral act – 'mes lèvres puiseraient sa présence réelle' (I, 13) – by which the child Marcel, clinging to early fantasies, imagines that he can incorporate his mother into himself. Characteristically, however, his mother's comforting presence provides 'tranquillity' rather than excitement and carries with it merely 'le pouvoir de m'endormir' (I, 13). The magical substance of the kill is just a soporific, a tranquilizer.

Besides, the project of assimilation is fraught with difficulties. The volatile essence of the kiss, 'précieux et fragile' (I, 23) as it is, is always in danger of evaporating altogether, and it is necessary to protect it from an alien environment. There is always the threat of attack from outside. In fact, when Marcel is sent to bed without his kiss, he buries himself in his private sanctuary and, making sure that nothing can get in, proceeds to 'boucher toutes les issues' and 'fermer les volets' (I, 28). The staircase which he has to climb seems hateful to him, and its smell of varnish – another intangible substance – seems to be the disembodied projection of his own unhappiness, which in turn assaults him by invading his consciousness in a manner 'presque instantanée, à fois insidieuse et brusque' (I, 28). Again, this kind of animistic projection would be a paranoid delusion if it were not just (just?) a childish fantasy. Marcel imagines, here, that his emotions (one step more refined than medieval humors) take the form of those volatile essences that mean so much to him, but, as in the medical theories of shamans and their patients, the pain that he feels seems to him like an alien invader, something that penetrates his body. The pleasure of drinking in his mother's attention is counterbalanced by the fear of being poisoned by the smell of varnish. In either case, the mechanism (assimilation or invasion) is the same: oral desires and paranoid fears of invasion are two sides of the same coin.

Because the kiss itself is so fragile and precarious, Marcel concentrates his thoughts and chooses exactly 'avec mon regard la place de la joue que j'embrasserais' (I, 27). How different is this from 'cette attention des maniaques qui s'efforcent de ne pas penser à autre chose pendant qu'ils ferment une porte, pour pouvoir, quand l'incertitude maladive leur revient, lui opposer victorieusement le souvenir du moment où ils l'ont fermée' (I, 23)? Like these madmen, Marcel is careful to shut the door not only to his room but to his mind, keeping out all distracting thoughts as if they were dangerous foreign substances. This careful, punctilious, obsessive concern is a defense against the terrifying unpredictability of what other people might do. Marcel is so obsessive that thoughts may enter his mind only on the condition that they leave behind any affective quality, even beauty. Here again he strives for the condition of a patient under an anaesthetic, who 'assiste avec une pleine lucidité à l'opération qu'on pratique sur lui, mais sans rien sentir' (I, 24). Feeling is dangerous, pure thought safe.

Significantly, the madmen cling to the recollection of the moment which obsesses them, the memory which they can hold onto and possess. In the same way Marcel holds onto the thought of the kiss, which is even more insubstantial (but less fleeting) than the kiss itself. Only he employs anticipation rather than recollection, fixing his thoughts on the future and so avoiding the terrifying 'abîme' (I, 24) of the empty present. He even hopes that his mother will come as late as possible, postponing the time when she will have to leave him but also prolonging the time in which she hasn't yet come. In this way he substitutes pleasurable anticipation for anxiety, finding it easier to control his own expectations than to control his mother's actual comings and goings.

Indeed, the moral of the story is the need for self-control. When his father, whose dictates seem arbitrary and unprincipled, and who has been cast in the role of the oedipal bogeyman, tells his mother to spend the night with him, Marcel's rigid system of defenses against anxiety collapses like a house of cards. He feels he has been rewarded for the cardinal sin of yielding to a nervous impulse, of giving in to a childish need. His mother and grandmother had wished to make him more self-reliant, less dependent on them, but now he is also dependent on the whims of 'un état nerveux' (I, 38) for which he is not responsible. When he is alone with his mother he cries without stopping – because of his nerves, says his mother, for no reason at all – not because he is seriously unhappy but because he can now give in to the emotions which threatened to overwhelm him. However, the idea that he has been freed from responsibility is an illusion. His sense of guilt is so basic that he feels he has betrayed his mother, failed to live up to her ideal, and forced her to stay with him against her will (which he has). The fulfillment of his wishes (the victory over his mother) is so fraught with guilt that he wishes his mother would go away again, leaving him to nurse his unhappiness in peace.

It is not only the denial of his wishes which troubles him but also their fulfillment. The rigid control which he exercises over his own thoughts – keep out all distractions, think of the future, concentrate on the exact spot – has become, in classic obsessional fashion, a new source of pleasure, safer and less threatening than the original desire. By keeping out all distractions, he defends against anything that might attract him, anything 'beautiful' like the pictures of the magic lantern, clinging only to a carefully circumscribed image. In short, Marcel needs no training in self-control: both before and after his father's miraculous concession, he fears (and feels guilty about) giving in to desires over which he has no control. Now he can cry without feeling guilty, as he suggests, but (to overstate the case) can he enjoy anything except tears, except his nervous condition itself, except the unhappiness which has become for him the sole condition for happiness? In fact, late in *Du côté de chez Swann,* his nervous excitement at the prospect of traveling to Florence and Venice makes him sick, preventing him from making the trip (I, 393). The imminent fulfillment of his desires arouses too much anxiety, but his anxious excitement has almost become an end in itself.

The little drama of going to bed, a 'screen memory'[5] which condenses the entire history of Marcel's uneasy and ambivalent dependence on his mother, a 'myth' which gives us the history of Marcel's childhood in a nutshell, confirms him as a kind of premature invalid not too different from his aunt Léonie. She too takes a somewhat masochistic satisfaction in her own suffering, spending her remaining days in bed 'dans un état incertain de chagrin, de débilité physique, de maladie, d'idée fixe et de dévotion' (I, 49). The amazing point about Léonie's illness is that, no matter how ambiguously psychosomatic, hypochondriacal, 'neurasthenic,' or simply imaginary it may be, it leads, in fact, to death. The implicit comparison between Léonie and Marcel makes him seem an old and eccentric neurotic like her, but it also suggests that the source of his complaint, like hers, is the fear of death, or in other words that the condition from which he suffers is life itself. Aunt Léonie's aim seems to be to cultivate an illness over which she at least has some control, to remain bedridden by her own choice, as if she were willing to be an invalid forever as long as she didn't ever actually have to die. So she detests two categories of people: those who urge her to live a more active life (denying the seriousness of her illness), and those who believe that she really is as ill as she says, turning a harmless fantasy into grim reality. In much the same way, Marcel wants his parents to commiserate with him in his suffering, to take it seriously, without actually giving in to him and so putting an end to his misery. But Léonie's illness, growing out of control, proves fatal, and Marcel's nervous complaint – that indefinite, fantastic, imaginary, neurotic condition of grief and anxiety which for centuries was called 'melancholia'[6] – turns out to be real. In her completely moribund life Léonie attaches 'à ses moindres sensations une importance extraordinaire' (I, 50), and finds in 'les occupations les plus insignifiantes de sa journée, concernant son lever, son déjeuner, son repos' (I, 118), an extraordinary value and interest. Yet this kind of minute, obsessive interest in trivial things, especially one's own sensations, which seems so neurotically self-centered, is exactly what makes Marcel's narrative – that is to say, Proust's novel – possible.

The experience of the madeleine, in which a whole world of memory opens out from a cup of tea, is a case in point. The sensation Marcel has is one of intense pleasure, a kind of 'puissante joie' or manic exhilaration which had rendered 'les vicissitudes de la vie indifférentes, ses désastres inoffensifs, sa brièveté illusoire'(I, 45), but it presupposes the sense of loss which has become second nature for Marcel, in this case the loss of his own past. The crumbs of cake dissolving in the warm tea become less material, less substantial; the smell and taste of the tea-soaked madeleine are even more impalpable, like the volatile essence of his mother's goodnight kiss; and this precious essence seems to fill the void within him. Still, no matter how volatile and insubstantial they may seem, Marcel's 'essences' are not abstract Platonic ideas, but rather magical, even imaginary, agents of the outside world. In Marcel's 'primitive' animism, the distinction between matter and 'spirit' has no real meaning. And yet he claims that the essence which fills him is already simply *himself* (I, 45). The taste of the madeleine is important to him only because it revives a memory (aunt Léonie's Sunday tea), a visual image conjured up like the projection of a magic lantern. New and unexpected events are normally a source of anxiety for Marcel, but this event turns out to be familiar, a repetition of something he has already experienced. And this unconscious familiarity is the source of his sudden pleasure, the realization that the world is inside him, that his childhood is not lost, and that life can't hurt him the second time around. The whole world of Combray seems to solidify, take shape, and assume material reality in Marcel's cup of tea, reversing the process of distillation into impalpable essences, seeming to belie the fact that these shapes and figures are only the insubstantial projections of his imagination.[7]   Part of the pleasure of the madeleine is that it *is* sudden and unexpected, temporarily mysterious and inexplicable, and in his walks along the two 'ways' out of Combray, Marcel seems to discover, after all, a pleasure in things outside of himself, in nature. He admires the hawthorn-blossoms arrayed on the altar of the local church precisely because they are alive, part of nature (I, 112), but he describes the hawthorn that he meets on the road in terms of the architecture of a church: 'La haie formait comme une suite de chapelles . . . que si j'eusse été devant l'autel de la Vierge... style flamboyant . . .' (I, 138). He is attracted by what is alive and spontaneous, but in order to possess it he has to place it in an artificial, aesthetic context, as if it were manmade after all. The very act of description – even if it is the narrator's, not little Marcel's – is a way of putting the flowers into his own terms and thereby making them his own. He frames the scene in a window – 'le soleil posait à terre un quadrillage de clarté, comme s'il venait de traverser une verrière' (I,138) – and he also paints a verbal picture, transforming 'live' flowers into a carefully composed arrangement of words.

He struggles to possess the secret of the hawthorns, if not to make the flowers part of himself then to fall into their rhythm, to attach himself to them in a passive submission to their mysterious and beautiful life. The struggle seems to be in vain, and the sentiment which the hawthorns arouse in him remains as obscure and vague as (at first) the sentiment aroused by the taste of the madeleine. But his strategy, significantly, is 'to lose' and then 'to rediscover' (I, 138) the odor of the hawthorns – 'devant les aubépines comme devant ces chefs-d'oeuvre dont on croit qu'on saura mieux les voir quand on a cessé un moment de les regarder' (I, 139) – just as, through no design of his own, he had to forget the taste of the madeleine in order to rediscover it, in order to enjoy it. Marcel can't possess something without in some sense losing it first, without leaving himself open, temporarily, to the mystery and uncertainty which frightens and attracts him at the same time – a capacity akin to what Keats called, a little obscurely, 'negative capability.' This preliminary renunciation is an escape from his characteristically intense, obsessive concentration on the source of his pleasure, an attempt to free himself from the strenuous, fatiguing effort of possession, a rather controlled attempt at letting go. But this is only a first step: Marcel recognizes 'la lâcheté qui nous détourne de toute tâche difficile' (I, 46), particularly his own, but he will not be satisfied until he has possessed the secret of his own enjoyment, the key to the mystery. This intellectual need to analyze his own feelings is incompatible with a naive acceptance of mysterious forces, but Marcel is not content to experience even pleasurable emotions uncritically.

And he comes closer to capturing the true quality of the hawthorns when his grandfather shows him another one, similar and yet different, like a new work by a favorite painter, new and yet familiar like the taste of the madeleine. This new hawthorn is pink instead of white, which Marcel compares to pink biscuits and pink cream cheese tinged with strawberries, as if the flowers too were not only colorful but edible. The narrator seems to be saying that children view beautiful things as an almost literal feast for the eyes – 'même lorsqu'ils ont compris qu'elles ne promettaient rien à leur gourmandise' (I, 140) – and in his effort to possess it Marcel too can almost taste the beauty of the flowers. In the same way the buttercups along the Guermantes way are 'jaunes comme un jaune d'oeuf' (I, 167) and even more beautiful because he can't actually consume them.

Indeed, in Marcel's eyes women as well as flowers are mysterious, beautiful, distant creatures whom he would like to possess but into whose world he cannot even penetrate. Making no distinction between 'la terre et les êtres' (I, 157), he longs for a peasant-girl who will rise up and let him embrace her, an imaginary wood-nymph who embodies for him the secret beauty of the Roussainville woods and of the whole natural world. This peasant-girl is vague and anonymous not only because she represents everything sensual and alive which Marcel can't quite reach – even the madeleine seems 'grassement sensuel sous son plissage sévère et dévot' (I, 47) – but because she exists nowhere except in his imagination. Accordingly, the peasant-girl never appears and his unsatisfied desire for her leads only to guilt-ridden masturbation. Marcel's peasant-girl is like the woman in his dreams in the opening pages of the book, a fantasy which he keeps chasing forever (I, 4-5). He comes to realize that his peasant-girls are 'les creations purement subjectives, impuissantes, illusoires' (I, 159) of his imagination (which makes him lose interest in nature), but this unsatisfied desire for an impossible object, an emotional attachment to something that is inside him and beyond him at the same time – a feeling which he applies, in the space of a few pages, to the lady in pink, Gilberte, Mme de Guermantes, and the hawthorns themselves – is what he calls love.

So, for example, he is at first disappointed by the disparity between the actual appearance of the Duchesse de Guermantes in church and the fantasy figure of his dreams, as different as 'la présence matérielle d'une actrice vivante' and 'une simple projection lumineuse' (I, 175). But he quickly reconciles his fantasies with the image that he sees, and though he can never hope to meet her, he can carry away and incorporate into himself the memory of her face. Indeed, the Duchess is for him an image of visual beauty, like the hawthorns, one which momentarily paralyzes his imagination and fixes his sight. Unlike the hawthorns, however, she looks back, glancing around the church and even at Marcel himself. Marcel compares the glance of her blue eyes to a ray of sunlight, blue light through a stained-glass window, as if that light were a quasi-material substance that he could absorb into himself. He imagines that she looks on him in a kindly, loving manner, but he falls in love with Gilberte even though – or rather, because – she looks on him (he thinks) with contempt.

That glimpse of her behind the hedge also virtually paralyzes him – because this kind of vision 'requiert des perceptions plus profondes et dispose de notre être tout entier' (I, 140) – and he looks at her with 'ce regard qui n'est pas que le porte-parole des yeux, mais à la fenêtre duquel se penchent tous les sens, anxieux et pétrifiés, le regard qui voudrait toucher, capturer, emmener le corps qu'il regarde et l'âme avec lui' (I, 141). This gaze is clearly a magical and aggressive instrument of possession, but her look, if not actually hostile, is subtle, ambiguous, inscrutable, as if she is not willing to admit that she sees him. (The gentleman that accompanies her, who turns out to be M. de Charlus, stares at Marcel with 'des yeux qui lui sortaient de la tête' (I, 141).) In order to make her see him and remember him, and in order to repay her comtempt in kind, Marcel would like to insult her, calling her hideous because she is so beautiful. His aim is to close the distance that separates them, to overcome her indifference, but that distance, that indifference, like the uncertainty inherent in his mother's goodnight kiss, seems like a necessary condition for his love. The somewhat masochistic need to suffer, like a Petrarchan lover, at the hands of a cruel and 'lordly' lady may soon turn into an angry, even sadistic desire for revenge, as in Marcel's wish to injure Gilberte, at least by denying the beauty that he cannot possess. Or, indeed, he may come to believe his expressions of hostility toward women – 'Comme je vous trouve laide, grotesque, comme vous me répugnez!' (I, 142) – and no longer find them beautiful. In the meantime the image of Gilberte, arrested and frozen in his memory, remains for him the 'premier type d'un bonheur inaccessible aux enfants de mon espèce' (I, 142).

If Marcel's adolescent attitude toward women can be reduced, ultimately, to his fantasy of anonymous peasant-girls, his attitude toward nature likewise owes a lot to his imagination. Near the end of the 'Combray' section he describes a kind of Romantic crisis of faith in which, like Wordsworth, he has lost that almost animistic childhood identification with the natural world: 'Soit que la foi qui crée soit tarie en moi, soit que la réalité ne se forme que dans la mémoire, les fleurs qu'on me montre aujourd'hui pour la première fois ne me semblent pas de vraies fleurs' (I, 184). The resolution of that Romantic crisis might come through a recognition that the childlike faith which creates an animate world is the individual's own (imagined) power of imagination, but for Marcel this problem is intimately linked with the impression that visual images (in particular) make on him.[8] Even his spontaneous outburst of joy when the sun comes out after a rainstorm ('Zut, zut, zut, zut') receives its immediate inspiration from the *reflection* of a pink-tiled roof in a pond, which he interprets (in the style of pathetic fallacy) as 'un pâle sourire répondre au sourire du ciel' (I, 155). Of course he too is smiling at the now-sunny sky, but it is the reflection, not the roof or the pond or the sky itself, which moves him most. The images of the magic lantern disturb Marcel, at first, because of their 'intrusion of mystery and beauty,' but the transformation of reality into mysterious, beautiful, fantasy-rich images is just what he has in mind.

By the same token Marcel's grandmother, in her commitment to aesthetic values, dislikes photographs because they are too literal and realistic, and would like to insulate Marcel from their vulgar reality by introducing 'plusieurs "épaisseurs" d'art' (I, 40). Instead of a photograph of some picturesque scene, she tries to give him a photograph of a painting of that scene. Something is lost in this substitution of art for reality – 'L'idée que je pris de Venise d'après un dessin de Titien qui est censé avoir pour fond la lagune, était certainement beaucoup moins exacte que celle que m'eussent donnée de simples photographies' (I, 40-1) – but something is gained as well, namely the personal, human quality which we assimilate into ourselves much more readily than the alien, impenetrable, inhuman surface of ordinary objects (cf. I, 84-5).

So Marcel loves the old church of Saint-Hilaire at·Combray, which he describes in long and affectionate detail, not because it is conventionally beautiful or artistic, but because it is natural, alive, human. From the point of view of primitive, mythical 'religion,' the whole universe is natural, alive, and anthropomorphic, but for Marcel these qualities are an essential criterion of beauty. The 'matière inerte et dure' of the memorial stones has melted into something softer and sweeter, like honey (I, 59), and the church itself is Marcel's familiar neighbor (I, 62). The stained-glass windows, illuminated images like the projections of the magic lantern, particularly appeal to him because they seem to use the natural light of the sun to outdo nature. The windows are most brilliant on dull days, and even when the earth outside is still bleak and barren they blossom like a 'tapis éblouissant et doré de myosotis en verre' (I, 60). The many colors of the church tapestries melt into one another like the stones which time has made 'couler comme du miel hors des limites de leur propre équarrissure' (I, 59). This Impressionistic dissolution of boundaries, this melting out into forms more fluid and diffuse (like the 'perfume' of the tea-soaked madeleine) has a seductive appeal for Marcel because it suggests that the boundary between himself and the outside world is not as rigid and impenetrable as he fears. Windows themselves are an ambiguous boundary, and semi-opaque, stained-glass windows, which let light in but do not let you see out, are more ambiguous still, which is one of the reasons why Marcel likes them.

The church seems so friendly and familiar, so much like home, and yet, paradoxically, it preserves the sense of difference, separateness, otherness that we have just denied. The wall of the apse, pierced with small windows at a great height (like eyes), seems more appropriate to a prison than a church. Besides this physical barrier there seems to be, between the church and the neighboring buildings, between it and everything else in Combray, 'une démarcation que mon esprit n'a jamais pu arriver à franchir,' 'un abîme' (I, 62,63). So there is a fixed boundary after all. The lofty steeple of Saint-Hilaire, which seems not only natural but also 'human' – 'si mince, si rose, qu'elle semblait seulement rayée sur le ciel par un ongle qui aurait voulu donner à ce paysage, à ce tableau rien que de nature, cette petite marque d'art, cette unique indication humaine' (I, 63) – puts the problem in clearer relief. Marcel's grandmother likes the curious old face of the steeple and even imagines it playing the piano, but this quaint anthropomorphism belies a deeper and more alien kind of consciousness. Though the old stones of the steeple seem softened and sweetened (like the stones in the church) by the light of the setting sun, they also seem 'tout d'un coup montées bien plus haut, lointaines' (I, 64). The cries of the birds circling around it likewise 'semblaient accroître son silence, élancer encore sa flèche et lui donner quelque chose d'ineffable' (I, 65). The image which moves Marcel so deeply is precisely that of a Gothic church steeple rising abruptly above a line of rooftops, breaking the line of sight, leaving ordinary human reality – and human language – far behind (I, 66). The familiar human quality of the church is only the last term in a complex emotional series which begins with the sudden, unexpected, epiphany-like appearance, taking one by surprise, of a naked spire on the horizon. The sudden appearance of what is new and unfamiliar is, as we have seen, fraught with anxiety for Marcel, but the conversion of this alien, threatening reality into something old and familiar – as in the case of the madeleine – creates intense joy. In short, the Gothic steeple of Saint-Hilaire, its lofty, impersonal otherworldliness stamped with a human face, fills him with the same kind of pleasurable anxiety as the magic lantern. As Marcel experiences it, beauty is a surprising, disturbing, potentially hostile force which has to be domesticated, made familiar, made human, an 'imaginary' foreign substance which he takes into himself in small, homeopathic doses.

The single spire of Saint-Hilaire and the two spires of Saint-André-des-Champs nearby form a progression that leads to the multiple image of three steeples (two at Martinville and a third at Vieuxvicq) converging on the horizon. The movement of the carriage in which Marcel is riding, along a winding road, creates a shift in perspective, causing the steeples to appear and disappear, to separate and converge as in a Cubist painting. Here again the setting sun seems to 'jouer et sourire' on the steeples, bathing them with light before they finally vanish in the darkness, reminding us of Marcel's almost primitive faith in the virtue of sunlight, which illuminates the phenomenal world and wards off the fear of total dissolution that darkness implies. The apparent motion of the steeples plays tricks with Marcel's sense of time and space, the churchtops appearing immobile or simply slow, lagging behind, but also suddenly springing into position 'par une volte hardie.' In fact he is astonished when the carriage arrives in Martinville much sooner than he expected, the steeples flinging themselves 'si rudement' in front of the carriage 'qu'on n'eut que le temps d'arrêter pour ne pas se heurter au porche' (I, 181). The impression (allowing for a touch of hyperbole) is of a dangerously unstable, animistic, *Alice in Wonderland* universe, 'prescientific' or simply post-Einsteinian, everything whirling in space, nothing fixed.

If objects are unpredictable, ready to spring up out of nowhere and strike at any time, the merger of the three steeples into one – and even into none, swallowed up by the (usually alien) darkness – seems reassuring, resolving the problem of sudden, even violent motion in a closing image of stasis and rest. Marcel softens the bold outline of the steeples by imagining them as his favorite images of beauty, first flowers and then maidens, 'charming and resigned,' whose motion is no longer violent but now timid and even *gauche.* The collapse of boundaries may create anxiety – especially if it is too sudden, like Marcel's headlong plunge into the church – but the gradual merger of the steeples creates that sense of unity, harmony, and stasis that Stephen Dedalus, in Joyce's *Portrait of the Artist*, prescribes for an image of beauty. Except that merger, in which the image loses its integrity, its clear outline, and fades out into the night, is not what Stephen has in mind. Stephen's idea of the aesthetic image is something clear and sharp, but Marcel likes the subtle play of fading light, the slow fusion and confusion of forms. It is important to remember, however, that if Marcel's 'plaisir spécial' ends with an image of rest and resolution, it begins with the sense of sudden, surprising change, the anxious discovery of a universe that is unpredictable and alive. Here again the experience is an exercise in controlled anxiety, like a ride on a roller coaster. Marcel fears the unpredictable, uncontrollable quality of life itself, but he needs to be reminded of it in order to feel alive himself.

Even a roof, a gleam of sunlight, the smell of a road can give him the 'plaisir irraisonné' that he feels but doesn't quite understand, but the immediate sense-impression is only an outer husk which contains, like a secret treasure, the 'real' source and meaning of his pleasure. By the same token, he identifies this inexplicable pleasure as 'l'illusion d'une sorte de fécondité' (I, 179), a sense of fullness and intoxication in which he himself is bursting with life, and the act of transcribing his experience, putting it into words, is like giving birth to the mystery inside him: relieving himself of the steeples and what they conceal, 'comme si j'avais été moi-même une poule et si je venais de pondre un oeuf' (I, 182). To expel the mystery on this way is not exactly to explain it, the fragment that is born is not yet a work of art, but this 'delivery,' like the fertile, 'pregnant' feeling that precedes it, makes him happy.

The mystery Marcel takes in must be as insubstantial and diffuse as the 'perfume' of the madeleine or the volatile essence of his mother's kiss. And, indeed, objects of visual beauty lose their material character and are distilled, like the projections of the magic lantern, into their own immaterial images. In this case, the avenue of assimilation is not the mouth or even the nose (tasting, smelling, kissing) but the eye, and the transparent, immaterial substance that Marcel takes in is light itself, the light that these objects reflect. The church steeples are seen in sunlight (as in Impressionist paintings such as Monet's studies of Rouen Cathedral at different times of the day), hawthorns and girls are linked with color (pink and white), and the Duchesse de Guermantes seems to emit a ray of light. Marcel's vision sometimes seems to be an aggressive instrument, as when he tries to penetrate to the mystery beneath the surface of what he sees, but normally he is the passive recipient of the light that enters his eyes – the 'supernatural' light cast, for example, by the eyes of Mme de Guermantes. In fact, his visual fantasies bear a striking resemblance to the medieval legend or myth in which the Virgin Mary is 'impregnated,' through the eye, by a divine beam of light.[9]

For Marcel, too, as for the Impressionist painters, light is a magical, fertile, almost supernatural substance, the magical essence of the object, and the first stroke of daylight which wakes him up at the end of 'Combray' – 'le doigt levé du jour' (I, 187) – is the same quasi-phallic 'doigt de Dieu' (I, 66) which he sees in the Gothic steeple of Saint-Hilaire. There is a reversal of sexual roles here, in which Marcel plays the passive part of the Virgin Mother and the fertile, life-giving power emanates not only from a seemingly pre-Christian sun god but from high-born courtly ladies like Mme de Guermantes (who appears like a figure on a stained-glass window and seems to inspire almost religious veneration in Marcel) and ambiguously virginal girls like Gilberte (surrounded by flowers in the manner of a church altar). It is the caressing gaze of Mme de Guermantes that penetrates Marcel, the glimpse of Gilberte's pink-freckled face that fills him with love, but the intercourse between them is visual and at a distance. (Mlle Vinteuil's fantasy – attributed to her friend – of spitting in her father's face is an attempt to ward off his penetrating vision, but it also implies an act of intercourse.) He prefers this rarefied, desexualized, 'aesthetic' relation just because it is easier to control and possess a disembodied mental image than an actual person with a will of her own.

In its essential form, however, what intrudes upon Marcel and shatters his complacency is simply the 'beauty' of things – that is to say, the mysterious, spontaneous, uncontrollable life of an animistic universe. The muse that inspires him and fills him with joy is 'life' itself, the sheer unexpectedness that shakes him out of his chronic self-absorbed depression. This depression is a kind of living death, a sense of emptiness and 'not-being,' and the sudden impingement of outside reality 'fertilizes' him with new life. But just as light passes through a window without damaging it – his preoccupation with

windows, especially stained-glass ones, is also anticipated by medieval theologians[10] – Marcel, repeating the Immaculate Conception,
remains a 'virgin' when the light of the external object penetrates his
eyes. Even though the outside world threatens to invade and
overwhelm him, he manages to keep his boundaries intact, take
possession of the invader, and turn it into an aesthetic image,
virtually a creature of his own imagination. Indeed, just as the taste
of the madeleine causes an earlier memory to rise within him (the
crucial factor in the 'resurrections' of the final volume), Marcel
repeatedly says that the mysterious, exhilarating quality which
seems to lie hidden in the object really resides within himself. In this
way he denies the external origin of that fertile, life-giving
joy – 'Chercher? pas seulement: créer' (I, 45) – and, like a shaman,
appropriates for himself the creative power that seems to animate
the universe, a power that he both fears and envies.

The mysterious feeling which rises from the depths of a dark
region and must be brought to light (I, 45-6) has 'unconscious'
origins, seemingly inside oneself and yet somewhere else, inaccessible, and the light which will penetrate the mystery – a kind of inner
vision – is, in a sense, simply consciousness. (The mysterious essence
and the inner light are split versions of the single magical substance
that Marcel seeks to possess, and their union, like the union of present and past sensations, resembles another fertilization.) Marcel's
intense, obsessive concentration on the object – for example, the
exact spot on his mother's cheek where he intends to kiss her – does
not enable him to penetrate to the heart of the mystery, and so he
turns away or closes his eyes, shutting out all extraneous ideas
(I, 24,46,138,178) in an effort to concentrate better, with renewed
strength, but also because (like Wordsworth and Blake) he knows he
can see more clearly, into this sort of mystery, with the 'mind's eye'
than with the bodily one. The investigation of the mystery may
seem blind and fortuitous, an alternate relaxation and renewal of
conscious control, but the sudden recognition that he achieves
(when, for example, he recalls the original taste of the madeleine) is
not accidental. It is the result of a carefully controlled experiment in
'free' association.

Marcel's need to 'relieve himself' of his own powerful emotions, to
stand outside himself, implies a serious division within him between
thought and feeling,[11] between self-conscious awareness and actual
emotion, in which any emotion is felt as a dangerous intruder upon

the apparently calm, self-controlled surface of consciousness. His emotional life falls into the extended 'manic-depressive' pattern of the Romantics, in which the child's joy in the natural world, seemingly lost, is recovered in the more sophisticated form of imagination, the 'faith that creates' no longer dependent on the outside world. But, despite his joy in nature, Marcel's childhood is already neurotic and anxiety-ridden. The anxiety of separation and loss is succeeded by sudden joy, the illusion of fecundity, of a creative power within him, but just as he wishes his mother would go away again after she comes to spend the night with him, he must detach himself from his own pleasure and return to his original depressed, 'unemotional' condition. Like his aunt Léonie, Marcel is afraid of being overwhelmed by too much excitement, of losing control – it is just this uncontrollable quality which excites him – and so he must cool off his excitement by a renewed effort of self-consciousness and self-control. As we have seen, this too makes him happy, but this new happiness seems more like a sense of relief, renewed calm, the kind of tranquillity that even his mother's kiss seemed to promise.[12]

The Marcel of the Combray years seems to 'feel' so much, but it is just because he feels at the mercy of his feelings that he longs to feel nothing at all. The end result of this strategy might be complete autistic withdrawal, but instead, at the end of *Le Temps Retrouvé,* Marcel turns himself into the selfless artist who, like a pregnant woman who dies in childbirth, like his own self-sacrificing mother and grandmother, has no life of his own but creates a new, ongoing life out of his own imagination. Indeed, in this remarkably self-centered kind of self-effacement, the Proustian artist resembles the primitive shaman who functions on the borderline of his society, withdrawing from it like Proust into his corklined room, going off by himself so that he may be possessed by the forces that animate the universe but also so that he may take possession of them.[13] Needless to say, an analogy between an artist and a shaman should not be taken too far, but this child-artist's implicit belief in an animistic universe, his penchant for taking metaphors literally, his uncertainty about where the self leaves off and the 'world' begins, reflect a way of seeing things that is more 'magical' than 'scientific.' Moreover, as Lévi-Strauss points out, magical thinking, which assumes that nothing is accidental and everything has meaning, that the universe is orderly and logical, is not *un*scientific.[14] On the contrary, this 'science of the concrete' explains too much, if only because these primitive 'scientists' are afraid of leaving anything unexplained.

Freudian psychoanalysis is also a 'science' of the concrete, and if it too tends to leave nothing unexplained, that is because it seeks to explain not the structure of the universe, but the structure of magical thinking. In 'Combray,' Marcel appears as the victim of childish fears, of his own fantasies, but it is precisely his ambivalent faith in the 'magical essence' of things, in the mystery and beauty that disturb him, that will enable him to be an artist. Or, rather, it is by becoming an artist that he will *attempt* to allay his anxieties, to resolve his ambivalences, and to realize his fantasies – or at least to *pretend* that he has succeeded, to convince himself, to believe that it is true.

2 The 'economic' problem in Proust and Freud

Je t'écris dans une mélancolie bien grande. D'abord cet argent perdu (et j'en ai le soupçon volé car je me suis rendu compte qu'il n'était pas dans la poche percée) qui m'avait d'abord ennuyé prend des proportions fantastiques. Ce soir à travers le mal d'estomac, la soirée etc cela me poursuit comme un crime, envers vous, je ne sais. Enfin, je comprends les gens qui se tuent pour un rien. Plus de trente francs! Et à ce propos la chose la plus pressée à m'envoyer est de l'argent (envoie m'en beaucoup trop et je tremble que ce ne soit pas assez) car sans cela je ne pourrais pas revenir si je m'y décidais.

– Proust writing to his mother [1]

In this letter, in which he blames himself for losing money as if it were a crime against her, Proust seems to imply that he owes his life to his mother and that, wasting it and squandering it in idleness, like the money he has lost, he can never repay her. Nor can he be free of her; the only solution is to ask for more money – to gorge himself on money though it will not be enough to satisfy him – in order that he may return home if he wants to. And yet his great novel, despite its brilliant analysis of snobbery and social castes, seems, at first glance, to ignore the existence of – the necessity for – money. Indeed, the fashionable world that Proust describes seems to exist in an anachronistic social vacuum – non-political, non-economic – where feudal privileges still obtain and personages with defunct royal titles reign over now non-existent kingdoms. In fact, however, economic relations do appear in Proust's novel, in surprising, significant, and revealing ways.[2]

Like a character in a Balzac novel, Marcel tries to 'buy' love with gifts. He sells a porcelain bowl that had belonged to his aunt

Léonie for 10,000 francs in order to buy Gilberte flowers (!), but he catches a glimpse of her walking with a possible rival and squanders the money on other women instead. He tries to buy Albertine's fidelity with a yacht and a Rolls-Royce, and, after she leaves him, he picks up a poor girl on the street, takes her home, puts her on his knee, and sends her away after paying her off with a five-hundred franc note. Moreover, in a perverse outburst of generosity, he donates the furniture he has inherited from aunt Léonie to a brothel, transferring it from one matriarchal figure (his aunt) to another (the 'madam'), as if he were robbing one to pay off the other.[3]

Just as the *beau monde* conceals a semi-secret, almost Balzacian underworld of homosexuals like Charlus, who is equally at home in an aristocratic salon and in Jupien's brothel, so the salon and the brothel are in many ways analogous institutions. The mistress of the salon and the madam of the brothel are two sides of the same coin, like the courtesan and the *grande dame* that Odette plays in different stages of her career. Mme Verdurin herself, *patronne* and go-between, denies the charge that she runs a *maison de rendez-vous*. But there is a third social institution, which occupies only a small 'space' in the narrative, which seems so marginal and insignificant, and which nonetheless mediates between the other two, sharing many of their characteristics, becoming a microcosm of both private and public worlds: namely, the 'public' toilet, the 'little pavilion' in the Champs-Elysées. The attendant or mistress of the little pavilion turns her toilet into her own private salon, a parody of the *beau monde*. Françoise thinks she is a marquise down on her luck, Marcel's grandmother thinks she is as snobbish as a Guermantes, and she acts the part, offering some customers free places and, 'avec une férocité de snob,' refusing admission to others: 'Ce n'est pas le genre d'ici, ça n'a pas de propreté, pas de respect, il aurait fallu que ce soit moi qui passe une heure à nettoyer pour Madame. Je ne regrette pas ses deux sous' (II, 311). The 'marquise' has to clean up after the rest of the society, but she too looks down her nose at others, whom she considers dirty.

She prefers customers who are neat, punctual, reliable, and business-like, who turn bourgeois values into (anal) obsessions, like the magistrate who shows up every day at three, never makes a mess, and stays more than half an hour to read his papers 'en faisant ses petits besoins' (II, 310). The 'marquise' is like a mother who appreciates his success in toilet training. One day he doesn't come, not because he has died but because his wife has; the next he returns, punctual as ever, faithful to the mistress of the toilet. She is a businesswoman herself, charging admission to her little 'theater,' having to please her customers in order to receive their tips.[4] But she proves her independence from strictly economic motives by turning away customers and giving away free seats. For that matter, the idea of charging for the privilege of using a toilet suggests an unusually tightfisted, pennypinching, bourgeois society, one that forces people to pay for the necessity or even the pleasure of satisfying a bodily need. The clients of the 'marquise' pay her to do their dirty work, or at least to clean up after them, but the 'marquise,' who would seem to be in the role of alienated labor, maintains her dignity by playing the role of bourgeois shopkeeper or theater-manager or even, lording it over her customers, the role of the snobbish marquise. In this last role she may spurn economic profit but only to claim the social prestige that enables her to look down her nose at others.

Indeed, snobbery implies the need to shame others, to treat them like dirt and to make them feel dirty, 'untouchable' because they are unclean. This is not just a figure of speech. Mme Verdurin, turning against Swann, formerly one of the faithful, calls him 'cette sale bête' (I, 285), using the same expression that Françoise applies to the chickens she is strangling, turning the victim into a shameful (or shameless) scapegoat. Swann, in revulsion against the Verdurins, disgusted by their fetid gaiety and their nauseating jokes, decides to stop condescending to 'la promiscuité avec cette infamie, avec ces ordures' (I, 288). The aristocratic Charlus's 'wit,' like this jibe at Mme de Saint-Euverte, is scatological and sadistic: 'Je me dis tout d'un coup: "Oh! mon Dieu, on a crevé ma fosse d'aisances," c'est simplement la marquise qui, dans quelque but d'invitation, vient d'ouvrir la bouche' (II, 700). The lift-boy at Balbec thinks that the name Cambremer is really Camembert, a smelly provincial cheese, and the future Duchesse de Guermantes's joke that this insufficiently illustrious name ends too soon makes a double pun on the word of Cambronne, *merde*. This is the famous wit of the Guermantes. Moreover, to cite one more perverse example of the 'anal-sadistic' impulses that seem to be inherent in snobbery, the sister of the Balbec page-boy, who is the mistress of a rich gentleman, 'ne quitte jamais un hôtel sans se soulager dans une armoire, une commode, pour laisser un petit souvenir à la femme de chambre qui aura à

nettoyer. Quelquefois même, dans une voiture, elle fait ça . . .'
(II, 980). The page's sister gives us the principle behind snobbery,
even the reason for social inequality, in a nutshell: 'il faudra
toujours qu'il y en ait pour que, maintenant que je suis riche, je
puisse un peu les emmerder' (II, 980). Snobs turn up their noses at
those they take to be their social inferiors, but it is the snobs
themselves who create the bad smell, who try to rise above the
'gutter' by leaving their own 'dirt' behind them, projecting whatever
they consider shameful and dirty (in themselves) onto those
'beneath' them.

The economic transactions of the public toilet – to return to the
little pavilion in the Champs-Elysées – remind us of that other social
institution where people pay for the privilege of satisfying bodily
desires, the brothel, as if the 'marquise' were in fact a 'madam.' In
fact, since the 'marquise' lets him in free, Marcel wonders if she has
'du goût pour les jeunes garçons' (I, 493). The 'bathroom' in the
Champs-Elysées reminds us as well of the baths where Albertine
meets her lovers. These baths are the setting for the secret pleasures
that disturb Marcel so much, and the woman who presides over
them, who takes the lavish tips of Albertine and her friends, is
another 'marquise,' the madam in what has become a private
brothel. This bathing, like the river-bathing that Albertine engages
in with the laundress and her friends, may be conducive to erotic
games, but it is probably not 'accidental' that the girl is a laundress,
that the activities Marcel finds so sordid, so unclean, so shameful,
are associated with washing, bathing, and cleaning.

Moreover, the old, damp walls of the little pavilion emit a cool,
musty odor which, like the 'sweeter' fragrance of the tea-soaked
madeleine, gives Marcel a special pleasure, for the simple reason
that he has smelled it before. In this early example of spontaneous,
fortuitous recollection, the cold, humid, moldy, almost sooty smell of
the pavilion reminds him of his uncle Adolphe's room at Combray,
the one that is shut up after Marcel visits his uncle in Paris and
accidentally starts a quarrel between him and the rest of the family.
Even a 'trivial' impression, even a 'bad' smell, can fill Marcel with
happiness, with a sense of beauty. But this case of reminiscence is
somewhat unusual in that it is not as trivial as it seems: unlike most
of the others, it has a certain 'content.' The musty smell is linked not
only with the empty, shut-up room at Combray but with the room
in Paris where Marcel meets the mysterious lady in pink. The room

in Paris (like a room in a brothel) is the setting of an 'illicit' affair, frowned upon by respectable society and by Marcel's parents, who cause the other room in Combray to be closed to the social outcast, Adolphe. In other words, the slightly wet, slightly dirty odor of the little pavilion – signifying, in effect, the odor of the toilet – is also the odor of secret sensual pleasure, and this is another reason why Marcel likes to smell it.

The identification of the toilet with a scene of secret pleasure reminds us of the toilet at the top of the house in Combray where Marcel masturbates, which smells of iris and wild currants rather than anything 'worse.' Even here, sexual pleasure is associated with an underlying, seemingly innocent, sense of smell. After Marcel smells the musty odor of the pavilion – but before he identifies it – he has an erotic game of wrestling with Gilberte that apparently leads to orgasm. The wrestling leaves him out of breath, and soon, as if to confirm the warning that the gardens of the Champs-Elysées are not healthy for children, he comes down with a vague asthmatic or allergic illness that threatens to prevent him from going to play with Gilberte. Whether it has a psychological origin or not, the illness seems to be a punishment for the pleasure he has taken with her, but the 'punishment' of asthmatic choking fits corresponds more directly to Marcel's 'innocent' pleasure in breathing the fresh air of gardens or the stale, musty odor of closed rooms. Marcel likes both the fresh, clean air of the natural world, the world that he can see from the lofty toilet of Combray, and the musty odor of the toilet itself, of the closed rooms where secret pleasures are enjoyed. It is in the very same pavilion in the Champs-Elysées that his grandmother has her stroke, but the shameful quality of 'contracting' a disease in a public toilet – so incongruous in regard to Marcel's grand-mother – may apply more obviously to Marcel himself, for whom the pleasures of the Champs-Elysées evoke guilty feelings. He even worries (before he realizes what's wrong) that his grandmother, who has taken too long in the toilet, will shame them in the eyes of the 'marquise' by not leaving her a large enough tip, by appearing too *petit-bourgeois.* A big tip – a show of social prestige – could compen-sate for too much illicit pleasure.

The memory of uncle Adolphe's room, which the odor of the little pavilion evokes, is like a screen memory which conceals as much as it reveals. Marcel remembers the room in Combray but not, explicitly, the one in Paris; Adolphe himself, but not the lady in pink. He recalls the little room on the ground floor but not the one at the top of the house, although the latter is linked to the little pavilion by three signifying elements: it contains a toilet; it has a distinctive odor; and, like Adolphe's other room or like the gardens near the pavilion, it is a scene of sensual pleasure. Indeed, there is another unacknowledged (unconscious?) link between the scene in the Champs-Elysées and the house in Combray, for there is another *petit pavillon* behind aunt Léonie's house, which also opens onto a garden. And in the first, most famous example of 'unconscious' reminiscence, the case of the madeleine, the fragrant odor of Léonie's *limeflower* tea conjures up not only the image of the house with its pavilion but 'toutes les fleurs de notre jardin et celles du parc de M. Swann, et les nymphéas de la Vivonne' (I, 47) – in other words, all of Combray, town and gardens alike. The gardens of the Champs-Elysées are the scene of a sexual encounter, and in fact flowers are associated with sexuality throughout the *Recherche:* with Gilberte under a hawthorn-hedge, with the *jeunes filles en fleurs* of Balbec.[5]

In short, the pavilion/garden combination (Champs-Elysées or Combray), this indoor/outdoor scene whose ambiguous 'bad'/ 'good' smells signify for Marcel the pleasures of the body, the senses, the natural world, or life itself, is a crucial element in the underlying symbolic structure – the implicit 'chain of signifiers' – of the *Recherche.*[6] This complex symbolic space is like a Moebius strip in which inside and outside are reversible aspects of the same surface: whether looking out or looking in, Marcel feels cut off from forbidden pleasures. Indeed, this reversible symbolic space can, in a sense, be reduced to Marcel's own body, which is simultaneously a refuge from the outside world, a vantage-point from which to view it, and also itself an alien region of dangerous desires that demand to be gratified, so that his own alienated 'self' is still always on the *wrong* side. As Beckett's melancholy narrator says in *The Unnamable*: 'an outside and an inside and me in the middle, perhaps that's what I am, the thing that divides the world in two...'[7] But the pavilion/garden is also a social space, the place where Marcel and Gilberte, Marcel and the 'marquise,' Marcel and his aunt Léonie, Marcel and his grandmother, meet, where he can finally smell the flowers, where his desires might finally be gratified.

It is a psychoanalytic cliché that money is shit, or rather that money is unconsciously identified with a bodily product whose value in sensual pleasure is denied, repressed, reversed, and ultimately 'sublimated.'[8] Indeed, the symbolic connotations of money reflect the matter/spirit dichotomy so basic to Western culture: money is dirty, shameful, and 'materialistic,' but it also enables one to buy beautiful objects and 'rise' above the rest of mankind into a sublime, ethereal, fantasy-like world. This is what the page's sister seems to mean when she tells us that she needs people to shit on. But this strictly anal interpretation (even as an explanation of origins) seems too narrow and limited. The sooty, 'dirty' odor that Marcel finds so pleasurable seems to reflect the anal origins of valuable things, but Proust upsets the opposition between 'bad' and 'good' smells: the musty odor of the pavilion is inseparable from the sweet 'fragrance' of flowers or the 'perfume' of (limeflower) tea. By the same token, the 'higher,' more innocent, quasi-oral pleasures of smelling and tasting seem inseparable from the 'coarser' sexual pleasures that accompany them. And yet the former pleasures, so much more prominent in these scenes, seem to 'hide' the latter, which are barely indicated in ambiguous, euphemistic allusions:

> je la tenais serrée entre mes jambes comme un arbuste après
> lequel j'aurais voulu grimper; et, au milieu de la gymnastique
> que je faisais, sans qu'en fût à peine augmenté l'essoufflement que
> me donnaient l'exercice musculaire et l'ardeur du jeu, je répandis,
> comme quelques gouttes de sueur arrachées par l'effort, mon
> plaisir auquel je ne pus pas même m'attarder le temps d'en
> connaître le goût (I, 494).

The form or 'taste' ('goût') of the pleasure is not simply the ambiguous 'drops' ('gouttes') that Marcel produces; it is the recognition of what they are. Moreover, the odors and perfumes that Marcel breathes are barely material, barely substantial, impressions, which he must analyze and interpret in order to 'possess' them. Perhaps Proust's precious 'essences' – hidden 'within' the impression, 'behind' the visible surface of an object – imply a spirit/matter dichotomy after all, a Platonic hierarchy of values which identifies the true significance of an impression with its spiritual 'essence.' But 'spirit' and 'matter,' essence and impression, are finally inseparable in Proust's text, and the musty, earthy odor of the little pavilion emphasizes the inescapable 'materiality' of even the most rarefied and 'sublime' impressions.

In the place where Marcel breathes in dangerously pleasurable odors, he may or may not succeed in 'stealing' a kiss from Gilberte but he winds up *losing* his breath as well as the few drops of 'sweat' that he would prefer not to acknowledge. In his private *cabinet* at the top of the house in Combray, this breathless paroxysm of sexual pleasure makes him feel that he is risking his life in a dangerous, potentially fatal journey. Special odors 'inspire' Marcel in a rather literal way, but this pleasurable inspiration is counterbalanced by a loss of breath – or of bodily substances, in the garden or in the bathroom – that may seem to turn pleasure into 'fatal' self-punishment. It is significant, then, that in his erotic wrestling match with Gilberte, Marcel tries to steal back the letter he has given to her, the letter he has written to her father Swann in an effort to prove that his intentions are honorable and 'pure.' As Marcel admits, the wrestling match seems to belie the claim of the letter, as if that letter – delivered by Gilberte from her 'boyfriend' to her father and (almost) back again – had now become a token of sexuality, of the sexual favors that Marcel is trying to win from Gilberte. It is as though love – or sexual relations – were a delicate equilibrium in which each lover tried to wrest some prize from the other, some sign or proof of the other's love, to 'possess' that love, while at the same time fearing to deplete one's own supply of sexual pleasure, of 'breath,' or of life itself. In the simplest form of the economy of Proustian desire, one loses one's *breath* in the exciting/ exhausting effort to possess the forbidden odor associated with sensual pleasure, the magical 'spirit' or 'essence' of another person's life. And yet this forbidden fruit, whether it be 'spirit' or 'flesh,' may be represented, in the erotic game, by a *letter* which comes to 'mean' the opposite of what it 'says,' a letter written by oneself which betrays the very desires that one has denied, a letter 'belonging' to oneself which one has to attempt to steal back. Marcel does recover the letter and he does experience erotic pleasure, but he does not win Gilberte's love or her sexual favors: he is left, out of breath, with his own empty words and his own unfulfilled desires.

Freud himself, in complete separation from his anal theory of money, developed a sweeping, metapsychological, physical-science model of psychic energy or 'libido' which he called economic because it seemed to imply a kind of Benthamite calculus of pleasure and 'unpleasure,' in this case internal, unconscious, and automatic. Freud's 'pleasure principle' asserts that the total psychic energy in the system tends either to maintain its own homeostatic level (reducing unpleasurable increases in tension to zero) or to be reduced, itself, to zero (Nirvana principle). Thus, 'beyond' the pleasure principle of tension-release, we find the death 'drive' toward total energy loss.[9] In addition, Freud's 'economic' theory of narcissism requires him to assume an unstable equilibrium between 'object-libido' and 'ego-libido' – that is, between energy 'invested' or 'cathected' in others and in oneself, so that one can love others only by denying oneself love and that one inevitably loves oneself more if one loves others less.[10] But this 'economic' conception is less a principle of explanation than a symptom of a fear of loss, a fear whose origin might lie in a fantasy of a mother who, instead of feeding her child, drained its life instead. This is the fantasy in Blake's 'Mental Traveller' of the Woman Old who measures the life of a newborn babe, 'Just as a Miser counts his gold': 'She lives upon his shrieks and cries,/And she grows young as he grows old.' And isn't Freud's death drive, which implies an entropy-like tendency to run out of available energy and (as a result) die, essentially the myth of Balzac's *La Peau de chagrin,* which warns that the fulfillment of desire leads inevitably to death? Freud's libidinal energy – divided into ego-libido and object-libido – reflects a closed economy in which the 'energy' that I possess is opposed to the fulfillment of my desires, to the unfulfilled 'lack' that I desire to fulfill. I desire, finally, what I do not and cannot possess, and the life-sustaining energy that I do 'possess' becomes a kind of neo-Balzacian vital essence which substitutes for the absolute 'presence' that always eludes me. If my desires are 'satisfied,' my energy level is reduced, so that complete satisfaction is possible only when there are no more desires to be satisfied, no more energy to be 'released,' in the entropy-like movement of Freud's 'death instinct.' In short, despite its increasing awareness of negation, self-destruction, and death, Freud's 'economic' model of energy balance seems to betray the illusory metaphysics of presence and self-presence that Jacques Derrida finds in the whole history of Western thought.[11] 'Energy is eternal delight,' says Blake, but what *is* psychosexual energy?[12]

Paul Ricoeur has traced the interplay between Freud's 'energetics' and his 'hermeneutics' – between his neurobiological, quasi-physical metapsychology of drive and energy and his psychological, quasi-linguistic interpretation of dreams and symptoms – and Derrida has shown, in 'Freud and the Scene of Writing,' that even the early, physicalistic energy model gives way – in Freud's writings – to a 'graphological' model of differential memory traces, a model based on language and writing.[13] In 'La Parole soufflée' (word/speech stolen, spirited away), Derrida remarks that theft – the theft of private possessions or of bodily parts or even of the shit which may seem to have been stolen from one's body – 'is always the theft of speech or text, of a trace. The theft of a possession does not become a theft unless the thing stolen is a possession, unless it has acquired meaning and value. . . .'[14] In the Proustian economy of desire, Marcel's life-sustaining spirit/breath (*souffle*) is stolen or spirited away from him (*soufflée*) even as he tries to breathe in the odor of love and desire, to 'steal' the letter in his girlfriend's hands, to win her sexual favors. But as Proust, Derrida, and Freud would remind us, these signs have to be interpreted in the context of memory, of desire, of other signs. The 'marquise' of the little pavilion lets Marcel use her toilets for free, not making him pay for sensual pleasure, but in a certain sense Marcel may leave something behind for the 'marquise,' a gift of uncertain value, though not in the patronizing, snobbish fashion of the page-boy's sister.

Just as the *petite phrase* of Vinteuil's sonata and septet and the *petit pan* (the little patch of yellow wall) of Vermeer's painting become microcosms of their art, of different kinds of art, so too the *petite madeleine* dipped in tea seems to be a microcosm of Proust's own art, of the transformation of a trivial taste or odor into a newly-created world of flowers and gardens and houses. But there is another alliterative 'little phrase,' whose initials are also p, which represents the central 'scene' of Proust's economy – namely, *petit pavillon,* the little pavilion in the gardens of the Champs-Elysées. In the light of the name by which women like the 'marquise' are still called – *les dames pipi* – Proust's text might also seem to imply that the gift Marcel leaves behind him is simply, surprisingly *pipi* (urine), one possible linguistic condensation of all these little 'things' and little 'phrases' of the form p-p (the letters alone pronounced *pépé*): at once a material, quasi-sexual substance which Marcel produces out of his body, like the drops of semen in the game he plays with Gilberte, and at the same time a purely linguistic sign of an elusive 'presence' that may be translated into art. (Admittedly, this search for a missing signifier sounds rather farfetched, and my overall reading of Proust's novel does *not* depend on it. But there may be some value in pursuing apparently farfetched, unverifiable interpretations if they turn out to uncover significant *connections* in the text, the kind of unconscious connections that may be far removed from the conscious intentions of the author.)[15] Just as the madeleine links Marcel to his aunt and to his mother, 'pipi' may link the *petit enfant* to the motherly *dame pipi* who offers him his own toilet and helps him to satisfy his bodily needs. Perhaps the child-artist who creates 'pipi' may feel that he is demonstrating his own autonomous ability to create something all by himself (a work of art) while at the same time offering this token of uncertain value as tribute to the hidden overseer of his work, the mistress to whom he owes both his work and his life, his mother.

Neither the phrase *les dames pipi* nor the word *pipi* appears as such in Proust's text, but this 'missing' word is 'generated,' as it were, by the 'play of signifiers' in the text, by the context of associations, by the repetition of all those *petit* p's, by the assonance of (French) *i*-sounds in *petit* and *pavillon*, by the immediate context of the pavilion itself. In one sense, Proust's economy of desire and need is simply an economy of signs, of words and letters, that have no meaning and no value *except* in the context of this economy, of this circulation of signifiers which is represented in the text but which the text itself cannot completely 'contain.' Apparently missing from Proust's text, 'stolen' from Proust's discourse, the absurd, childish, yet potentially 'meaningful' signifier *pipi* is created not simply by Marcel who uses the bathroom, nor simply by the author who doubles and redoubles his p's (and i's), but by the metaphorical/ metonymical possibilities of the text itself. The *'parole soufflée,' pipi*, signifies the kind of quasi-material, quasi-sexual 'presence' (breath/ spirit/life) that every writer seeks to find in language, in the text he has written, but this missing, hidden (unconscious?) sign acquires meaning and value only in the 'economic' process of exchange, of circulation, of so-called 'dissemination.' Derrida's idea of an unlimited 'dissemination' of signifying traces, of an 'expenditure without reserve' in which the proliferation of signs would be endless and inexhaustible (without entropy), seems surprisingly like a neo-Romantic, neo-Balzacian myth not of 'presence' but of seminal, fertile power, located not in a person nor even in a text but rather in the chaotic, anarchic, fragmented, non-hierarchical, intertextual economy of signs (not *in* those signs but between them, in their relations to each other).[16] Of course Derrida's seminal 'dissemination' is metaphorical, but the very notion of 'dissemination' calls into question the dichotomy between literal and figurative meanings, between philosophical 'truth' and myth.[17]Near the end of his essay on the psychotic Dr Schreber, Freud admits that Schreber's spermlike 'rays of God' bear a surprising resemblance to his own theory of 'libidinal cathexes':[18] Freud's 'economic' model is not a delusion, but a better explanation of the 'economic' relations of need and desire would proceed from 'energetics' to 'hermeneutics,' from neo-Romantic myths of sexual energy to an interpretation of 'symbolic' exchanges.[19] In Proust's words: 'Sans doute ce déchiffrage était difficile, mais seul il donnait quelque vérité à lire' (III, 878) – whatever truth might be *read* in the process of interpretation itself.

3 Bonds of love and kinship

De relations qui ne sont pas consacrées par les lois découlent des liens de parenté aussi multiples, aussi complexes, plus solides seulement, que ceux qui naissent du mariage.

– III, 262.

Proustian love, which develops into an unstable compound of desire, jealousy, and hostility, grows out of a need to be loved. In the prototypical case, Marcel doesn't want to let his mother out of his sight and wishes she could spend the night with him. Absence seems to imply abandonment, and so, in order to be sure she really cares about him, he wishes he could control her life, bend her will to his own, hold onto her, possess her. Throughout the novel sexual possession is subordinated to this kind of psychological possession, this control over the other person. However, it seems that no one can ever really possess another person, and the lover is always beset by doubts and anxieties about the mysterious life the other person is leading when he is not around. Conversely, it is the mysterious opaqueness of the other person's life, its unpossessible 'otherness,' that makes her desirable, repeating on a different level the child's dependence on a mother who has a life of her own. This gap of 'otherness' between oneself and the other person is the necessary condition for love: one loves what one can't possess, one needs to maintain the gap that one is always trying to close. When his mother comes to spend the night with him, Marcel wishes she would go away again, partly because he is afraid of being overwhelmed by his own emotions but also because, making the best of an uncertain situation, he has already taken his own bitter-sweet longings as a substitute for real human contact. He would rather love at a distance, in his own imagination, preferring self-sufficiency to anxious dependence on another person. And a certain masochistic need to sabotage one's own love, in an effort to prove one's independence and make the other person, in turn, dependent on oneself, will emerge as an essential ingredient of Proustian love.

I

Indeed, the love affairs that Proust describes, especially Marcel's, draw on 'filial sentiments' in many crucial ways. The jealous suspicions that obsess Swann and Marcel – Proust gives them ample justification for their suspicions, but that is because, like them, he cannot believe in fidelity – grow out of the same sense of exclusion and abandonment that Marcel feels as a child, in his room, exiled from 'cette salle à manger interdite, hostile' which seems to be concealing 'des plaisirs malfaisants et mortellement tristes parce que maman les goûtait loin de moi' (I,30). As Marcel tells us in his capacity as narrator, Swann has experienced a similar anguish in his love for Odette, 'cette angoisse qu'il y a à sentir l'être qu'on aime dans un lieu de plaisir où l'on n'est pas, où l'on ne peut pas le rejoindre' (I, 30). The fact that Marcel cannot, at first, enter the houses of Gilberte and Mme de Guermantes, that he has no part in their lives, contributes to his love for them, but even when he shares the same house with Albertine he is troubled by the separate life she leads which he can never completely know. Swann, likewise, tries to convince himself that the time he spends with Odette is a 'real' part of her life, that the lamp, the armchair, the orangeade are not just theatrical properties but the real things, that the 'effroyable et surnaturel' world which she inhabits when he is not there is only a projection of his imagination (I, 298-9). The mysterious and unknown 'otherness' of the other person's life, which attracts one so much, is also terribly painful to bear. The jealous lover becomes obsessed by minute details of the other's life, clues to her infidelity – places she visits, letters she sends, names she lets slip – becoming a detective with an insatiable thirst for 'facts,' hard evidence which can substitute for the fleeting, intangible mystery that he can never actually possess. He seizes upon the slips she makes, inconsistencies in her story, apparently innocent words which have more than one meaning, as if he were either deciphering a difficult text or making one up out of his own obsessive associations, investing trivial details with a burden of personal meaning. This is the place of 'facts,' uncertain as they are, in Proust's unstable vision of reality, as clues and signs of a reality one can never be sure of.

Moreover, Marcel's own role in the narrative he comes to write is less that of an actor than an observer, an audience of one, a voyeur who spies and eavesdrops on the often unsuspecting performers: like the society novelist whose monocle serves as an instrument of psychological analysis and whose sole occupation is to observe. He loves to watch Albertine sleeping in bed, to lie down next to her and caress her defenseless body as if she were not a willing lover but a dead victim. This voyeuristic role is most obvious in the three parallel scenes where Marcel observes a pair of lovers, comparable to the 'primal scenes' in which a child observes his parents making love except that these lovers are, in each case, of the same sex: Mlle Vinteuil and her girlfriend at Montjouvain, Jupien and Charlus in the courtyard outside Marcel's house, Charlus and the man who beats him in Jupien's male brothel. Marcel, who once suspected Charlus of being a spy, wonders if Jupien's establishment is a meetingplace for spies. But it is he himself who is the spy, whose compulsive curiosity impels him to enter the establishment, prowl around the halls, and peer through a small oval window into someone else's room. In the case of Mlle Vinteuil, he claims that he could not leave without her hearing him, that she would have thought he had been 'caché là pour l'épier' (I, 159). In the case of Jupien and Charlus, after stumbling upon them accidentally he goes out of his way to spy on them, hiding in the vacant shop next to Jupien's and finally climbing a ladder in order to peep through a ventilator. In fact, he doesn't take the safe route through the cellar but goes right through the courtyard, 'comme si de telles révélations' – meaning the scene at Montjouvain as well – 'ne devaient être la récompense que d'un acte plein de risques, quoique en partie clandestin' (II, 608). He feels that he too, though he is only an observer, is doing something secret and dangerous, and this increases his pleasure. Besides, comparing this exploit to the duels he fought over the Dreyfus case (!), he admits he has nothing to fear except the possibility of *being seen* by the neighbors, as if (the voyeur observed) he might be caught in the act like Jupien and Charlus.

In all three scenes Marcel looks through a window, his favorite vantage point upon the world, the marvelous view from the top of the Paris house reminding us of the little closet (or toilet) at the top of his aunt's house in Combray, from which he looks out at the countryside and imagines peasant-girls rising up to meet him. In short, making a virtue of what seems like necessity, he prefers to take his pleasure at a distance, safely ensconced behind a window that enables him to see other people without their being able to see him. In an analogous scene, Swann posts himself outside a lighted window, thinking he will trap Odette and her lover, and discovers instead *two old gentlemen.* Marcel's voyeurism, like Swann's attempt to spy on Odette, reflects the obsessive curiousity of the jealous lover, the need to know what the other person is doing and the terrible anxiety of not knowing, the dizzying uncertainty about a secret reality that always remains hidden. The anonymous letter that Swann receives asserts that Odette has had other lovers, both men and women, and the fear that comes to haunt Marcel is that Albertine is a lesbian, that she has betrayed him with other women, including Mlle Vinteuil and her friend. He would like to spy on Albertine, to catch her in the act as he once caught Mlle Vinteuil, and the scene at Montjouvain takes on a new, personal meaning in his eyes, as though the friend of Mlle Vinteuil – or she herself – might have been Albertine.

The classic primal scene fantasy also suggests a betrayal, the oedipal betrayal of the child by one of his parents with the other. The scene at Montjouvain seems to reverse the primal scene, the daughter forcing her father to look on – magically present in his photograph – while she betrays him. (In still another parallel scene, Charlus tries to spy on Morel and the Prince de Guermantes in the brothel at Maineville while Morel, observing himself being observed, trying to play his part, has a better view of Charlus than he of him. Afterwards, at the Prince's villa, Morel is frightened out of his wits by a photograph of Charlus, who seems to be staring at him!) Ironically, Mlle Vinteuil behaves, at one point, like a daughter to her friend who plays the part of her mother, and yet M. Vinteuil himself had taken upon himself 'les soins de mère et de bonne d'enfant' (I, 159) for his daughter. The implication is not that Mlle Vinteuil is betraying her father for a 'mother' but that even her betrayal expresses a need to be acknowledged, to be loved, by a father, a mother, a loving parent. Indeed, like her friend, she does not mind that people will see them; she wants her father to see her, as if paying him back for some obscure betrayal from her childhood. In the prototype of these transformed 'primal' scenes, at the end of

Proust's early story *La Confession d'une jeune fille,* the mother looks on while the daughter, violating her mother's wishes, embraces her (male) lover: the mother dies from grief and the daughter, like the matricidal 'hero' of 'Sentiments filiaux,' prepares to commit suicide.

If we superimpose these scenes upon each other, we find a common structure with interchangeable roles:[1] Marcel witnesses what might be his own betrayal, like a child observing his parents making love, but we can imagine him playing the part of the *jeune fille* in the story of Mlle Vinteuil at Montjouvain, 'profaning' the memory not of his father but of his mother, whom he still loves, betraying her with another because he could not have her for himself. Of course this reading is reinforced by the *extra*textual evidence of Proust's homosexuality and of his own erotic rituals of profanation in which he 'abused' his mother's photograph.[2] Marcel calls homosexuals 'fils sans mère, à laquelle ils sont obligés de mentir toute la vie et même à l'heure de lui fermer les yeux' (II, 615): the 'profanation of the mother' that Marcel speaks of might be the son's last, perverse attempt to win his mother's approval. Mlle Vinteuil's friend threatens to spit on the photograph, but this is not just an act of hostility, of 'sadism': when Charlus spits into a young man's face, as he almost does to Marcel, he feels relieved, calmed, as if through this 'violente semonce' he had satisfied his desires after all (II, 629).

Marcel has wanted his mother to spend the night in his room, and in the strange, unfamiliar hotel room at Balbec, after lying in his grandmother's arms like a baby at the breast – 'Quand j'avais ainsi ma bouche collée à ses joues, à son front, j'y puisais quelque chose de si bienfaisant, de si nourricier, que je gardais l'immobilité, le sérieux, la tranquille avidité d'un enfant qui tète' (I, 668) – he would like her to do the same. Fortunately the partition is thin and her bed is just on the other side of the wall. Significantly, the vacant shop next to Jupien's (Marcel's secret vantage-point) is separated from it by a thin partition *(cloison mince)* just like the one at Balbec. It is as if Marcel imagined himself living by himself in an empty, unfriendly room separated from his parents' by a thin partition, wishing to see into that other room and observe what they were doing. If he cannot see, perhaps at least he can hear: the mouselike scratchings that he makes on the wall in order to signal his grandmother suggest that he is copying similar furtive noises from the other side, the noises of a person 'qui se remuait dans le lit, qui faisait tous ses manèges' (I, 669). For that matter, the mouse would like to be on the other side performing his tricks, and in his discussion of the 'Sodomites' Marcel describes hermaphroditic flowers in which 'l'organe mâle est séparé par une cloison de l'organe femelle' (II, 627), as Marcel is from his grandmother.

The photograph of the dead father Vinteuil, who as a ghostly presence witnesses his own 'profanation,' might be compared to the photograph of Marcel's grandmother taken shortly before her death, which reminds him of his cruel insensitivity toward her. She wants to leave him a picture in which her face is not yet ravaged by illness, but he ridicules her for what he takes to be her coquetry, her childish vanity. After her death his mother cannot bear to look at this photograph, because it *fails* to hide the signs of disease, as if it were a photograph not of her but of her illness, as if the camera could see what Marcel failed to see. In a similar but opposite way, Marcel carries around inside him, 'developed' and 'printed' in his memory, images of 'primal' scenes which he has never actually seen – which his imagination, like a fabulous X-ray machine penetrating that thin partition, has recorded anyway – scenes which, in various changing forms, he can't help seeing over and over again.

II

Marcel loves Mme de Guermantes, but also Gilberte and Albertine, because they seem to be unattainable. Gilberte's apparent indifference toward him, the gesture of contempt that she seems to give him when he first sees her, make him love her all the more. In fact, love develops into a seesaw oscillation between indifference and need: the other's indifference, real, feigned, or imagined, provokes one's own need to be loved, while the return of the other's love makes one love her less. By the same token a love like Swann's may begin in complete indifference but, through frustration, jealousy, or fear of betrayal, as in Marcel's case too, it can grow into an intense need. Love, then, becomes a battle of wills, of egos competing for domination and control, and the lover tries to make the other person love him by feigning indifference, an indifference which eventually becomes real, so that one's love is returned when one is no longer in love. Marcel's 'failure of will' in begging his mother to stay with him is also an assertion of will, an attempt to assert his authority over his mother. When she gives in to his demands, he has won a 'victory' over her which is a defeat for himself insofar as he cannot master his own needs. His feeling that he would be better off alone reflects a desire for self-control but also for control of his mother, whom he would like to summon and dismiss as he pleases. He is pretending to himself that he does not need her.

Swann really falls in love with Odette on the night that he arrives late at the Verdurins and finds that she is no longer there. He ransacks the streets of Paris looking for her: love begins

> quand – à ce moment où il nous fait défaut – à la recherche des plaisirs que son agrément nous donnait, s'est brusquement substitué en nous un besoin anxieux, qui a pour objet cet être même, un besoin absurde, que les lois de ce monde rendent impossible à satisfaire et difficile à guérir – le besoin insensé et douloureux de le posséder (I, 231).

And, indeed, his love is gradually transformed into painful jealousy, so that he takes a lighted window as a sign, as evidence, of Odette's infidelity and it turns out to be the wrong window. By the same token, Marcel is bound to Albertine by the pain of jealousy and doubt, not by a positive desire: 'Elle était capable de me causer de la souffrance, nullement de la joie' (III, 28). He is indifferent to her when she seems willing to live with him, but when he is most convinced of his own indifference, she suddenly abandons him, reawakening his desperate need for her. As with Gilberte, Marcel coolly, calculatingly pretends to break with her, in order to force her hand, to make her dependent on him, but he ends by actually breaking with her, losing her and also falling out of love with her: 'comme certains nerveux, pour avoir simulé une maladie, finissent par rester toujours malade' (I, 633).

Marcel sabotages his own love in order to strengthen it but also to forestall being betrayed, which seems inevitable: throughout the novel paranoid delusions of jealousy are amply corroborated by evidence of deceit and infidelity, both Odette's and Albertine's. Marcel needs to suffer in love, to feel he is being betrayed, because his childhood dependence on his mother has made unhappiness the condition of his happiness, doubt and uncertainty the conditions of his mother's love. This masochistic need to suffer, like his aunt Léonie's devotion to her illness, is accompanied by a corresponding desire to make someone else minister to one's suffering, an essentially sadistic desire to make another person suffer instead of oneself. Léonie, who is utterly helpless and dependent, is also a tyrant who puts everyone at her beck and call. Fearing her own death, she would like to imagine the rest of the family dying in some grand cataclysm so that she could enjoy the bitter-sweet pleasure of mourning for them. Because she depends on Françoise (her servant) so much, she fears she is betraying her, and in order to forestall actual betrayals she invents imaginary ones. Going one step further, she sides with her friend Eulalie against Françoise and with Françoise against Eulalie, suffering from paranoid suspicions which make her search for enemies to punish. Françoise herself, kind and devoted as she is, has a 'primitive' streak of sadism and cruelty which allows her to ignore suffering when it's close at hand, to hate her 'rivals' Eulalie and (later) Albertine, and to torture those who don't properly comply with her wishes, like the kitchenmaid and the chickens which she slaughters with cries of 'sale bête! sale bête!' (I, 122). One seems bound to develop a certain amount of hostility towards the person one loves because one is so dependent on that person; we want the other person to suffer for making us suffer. Marcel suffers from the 'nervous complaint' of his childhood, but he does his best to make everyone else, especially his mother, suffer too. When he grows up he becomes an irrational, paranoid tyrant who tries to make Albertine a captive in his own private, Marquis-de-Sade-like prison, allowing his paranoia to feed a petty kind of megalomania. In Proust's view of human relations, the master is dependent on the slave, but the master makes sure that the slave pays for the power the slave has over him.

In fact, 'sadism' of one sort or another is widespread among Proust's characters. The Verdurins ridicule Saniette, tormenting him as the scapegoat of their weekly rituals, fulfilling what seems to be a social need. After inviting Marcel to his room, the mercurial Baron de Charlus, appearing both violent and gentle, treats him with alternate contempt and affection. Presumably the contempt grows out of the affection, because Marcel has not shown himself sufficiently grateful for the Baron's overtures and because, unable to express his affection directly, the Baron is forced to cloak it in hostility. Indeed, Charlus quotes what might be the sadist's motto, 'qui aime bien châtie bien' (II, 559), implying that chastisement may itself be a form of love. But Charlus's mad rages also conceal what seems to be his most deep-seated source of pleasure, his masochistic desire to be beaten which is revealed late in the novel, in Jupien's 'brothel.' Sadism and masochism appear as complementary aspects of the same personality, as if, in his sadistic expressions of hostility, Charlus is simply adopting the other role in a reciprocal relationship where he was originally the suffering victim, identifying with the 'aggressor' and finding someone else to punish.[3] When he takes a sadistic delight in imagining Bloch beating his father, would he like to be that helpless father suffering at the hands of his son? Or would he rather be the son, punishing his own father for beating him? In Freud's acute essay 'A Child Is Being Beaten,' the beaten child, through all the permutations and reversals of fantasy, is finally oneself.[4] But who is doing the beating? Who is the original aggressor?

In a more subtle way Marcel, like Charlus, plays both sadistic and masochistic roles, suffering in love, loving his suffering despite himself, but also cruelly imprisoning Albertine, hounding her and spying on her, interrogating her, forcing her to live according to his own obsessional rules of silence and closed windows, treating her (as Charlus treats him) with alternate affection and indifference, if not contempt, a peculiarly refined version of psychological torture. After she expresses a willingness to return to him, he writes her a coldbloodedly sadistic letter insisting that they should not meet, in which he tells her that he will now keep for himself the yacht and the Rolls-Royce he has ordered for her, though he will never use them. Of course he is lying, carrying out a brilliant and thoroughly self-destructive strategy, hoping to make her return by urging her never to return. Marcel is venting his own frustration on the cause of his sufferings, on the 'aggressor' Albertine, attempting to reverse the roles, just as he might have wished to imprison his 'fickle,' unreliable mother in his own room, first to have her to himself and then, failing that, to punish her for being unfaithful. He attempts to control Albertine's comings and goings as he could never control his mother's, but in so doing he is playing a parental role, identifying himself with the one who lays down arbitrary rules and causes so much suffering in others. In his love for Albertine, at once 'filiale et maternelle' (III, 79), he becomes a strict parent trying to deal with a sensitive child, exchanging his customary role for the complementary one:

en regard de l'enfant sensitif que j'avais uniquement été, lui

faisait face maintenant un homme opposé, plein de bon sens, de
sévérité pour la sensibilité maladive des autres, un homme
ressemblant à ce que mes parents avaient été pour moi (III, 107).

In short, the original authors of suffering, whom the suffering
children, unsatisfied by masochistic compliance, or simply suffering
too much to enjoy it, eventually come to resemble, are their own
parents. They too become parents or, more neurotically, hostile,
paranoid sadists.

A clear illustration of the filial origins of this sadomasochistic
pattern of roles and identifications is the case of 'sadism' that Marcel
cites under that name, the case of Mlle Vinteuil. This 'sadism' is
more symbolic than literal: Mlle Vinteuil's homosexual friend
threatens to spit on the photograph of her dead father and the
presence of this photograph, 'looking' at them, seems to increase
their pleasure. Indeed, this photograph is subject to a kind of ritual
profanation in the black mass of their amorous relations, and
Marcel makes the point that this profanation, this violation of the
father's memory, would be meaningless – would not be a source of
pleasure – unless Mlle Vinteuil still, in some sense, loved her father: 'et
la vertu, la mémoire des morts, la tendresse filiale, comme elle n'en
aurait pas le culte, elle ne trouverait pas un plaisir sacrilège à les
profaner' (I, 164). Mlle Vinteuil may have 'killed' her father by causing
him so much grief, but her ritualized cruelty towards him, so diffident,
so innocent even, reflects the strength of her attachment to him, her
need for his presence, perhaps even her need to assuage her guilt over
hurting him by blaming him for it and taking it out on him.

Mlle Vinteuil may be out of her depth, a child playing at evil, but
several of the key characters in Proust's novel – Charlus, Morel, and
Marcel himself – share (in varying degrees) a kind of unstable,
temperamental, irritable, irrational, 'neurasthenic,' 'hysterical' kind
of personality, tending to replace tenderness and affection with
coldness and cruelty. In their irrational and hysterical moods these
characters give us the 'Dostoyevsky' side of Proust, to use Proust's
own metaphor, and Marcel's narrative of his life with Albertine
– a late addition tied to Proust's recent experiences – is a kind
of 'diary of a madman' which must be read as an ironic self-
portrait of a self-deluded narrator. However, Proust does seem to
be aware of his hero's 'madness.' Marcel says that it is hard to live
intimately with a madman and cites the example of Morel, who

accusait M. de Charlus de sa tristesse, sans pouvoir fournir
d'explications, l'insultait de sa méfiance, à l'aide de raisonne-
ments faux mais extrêmement subtils, le menaçait de résolutions
désespérées au milieu desquelles persistait le souci le plus retors de
l'intérêt le plus immédiat (III, 182).

Marcel adds: 'Tout ceci n'est que comparaison. Albertine n'était pas
folle.' But it is Marcel who is the master of subtle reasoning, the
egomaniacal champion of self-interest, and the hidden implication
is that, if Albertine is not mad, Marcel is!

Of course, as we have seen, there is a method in Marcel's
'madness,' a complex structure of identifications in which he
imagines himself reversing his mother's dominance over him and
plays the part of a cruel parent to Albertine. But despite this reversal
of roles, Marcel, from early experience, also identifies himself with
Albertine, the suffering victim. He has an anxious, uncanny pre-
sentiment of her death, which turns out to be accurate – in fact, like
Swann with Odette, he has wished many times that she would die in
an accident, which would take her off his hands – but after she
leaves him he has recurring thoughts of suicide, as if he could not
live without her and felt that she was taking his life with her. Suicide
offers a way of turning his vengeful, sadistic feelings on himself,
carrying through this split identification between murderer and
victim, but the motive behind this idea is self-punishment, a need to
expiate his own guilt. The tale of Marcel's run-in with the police,
after he picks up a little girl on the street to console him for the loss
of Albertine, reads like a miniature *Crime and Punishment:* Marcel is
branded a criminal, the police watch his house as he formerly had
Albertine watched, and it seems to him, his guilt outstripping his
rationality, that the charge of corrupting minors might include
Albertine also, that he has not lived chastely with her. In other
words, even if the charge is false, the guilt is well-deserved. Before,
Marcel's paranoia fueled his sadistic designs; now, new paranoid
fears seem to come true, as if to punish him for his guilt. The reason
he gives for contemplating suicide does not seem sufficient, but it
testifies to the depth of both his grief and his guilt:'cette impossibi-
lité de bercer jamais une petite fille me parut ôter à la vie toute
valeur à jamais,' and 'si j'avais pensé que même une petite fille
inconnue pût avoir, par l'arrivée d'un homme de la police, une idée
honteuse de moi, combien j'aurais mieux aimé me tuer!' (III, 446).

Murderous impulses seem inherent in the sadomasochistic ambivalences of love – Mlle Vinteuil has 'killed' her father, Charlus threatens to kill Morel – but once one has succeeded in getting rid of, in 'killing off,' the person one loves too much, these feelings return upon oneself in the form of guilt, grief, and thoughts of suicide. Indeed, Marcel frequently couples Albertine's death with his beloved grandmother's, and it seems to him, in an outpouring of guilt, 'que ma vie était souillée d'un double assassinat' (III, 496). His grief for each of them takes a parallel course in its attempt to achieve the complete oblivion which will leave him indifferent to their memory, except that the miraculous 'resurrection' of Albertine (in the misconstrued telegram from Gilberte) does not affect him, while the oblivion which overtakes him after his grandmother's death, his apparent inability to grieve for her, ends in a miraculous reminiscence of her, a realization of real grief. Marcel's guilt over his grandmother's death also seems too severe, but he feels that in making her obey the whims of a 'spoiled' child, in exploiting her concern for him, in failing to live up to her hopes, and in failing to see her own suffering – as when he accuses her of vanity in primping for Saint-Loup's photograph – he has been a 'jeune homme ingrat, égoiste et cruel' (II, 756). He recognizes that guilt and self-reproach play a crucial role in the feeling of grief: 'car comme les morts n'existent plus qu'en nous, c'est nous-même que nous frappons sans relâche quand nous nous obstinons à nous souvenir des coups que nous leur avons assenés' (II, 759). Even grief, therefore, may be self-centered, deriving its intensity from a kind of masochistic identification with the person we feel we have wronged: 'Je sentais que je ne me la rappelais vraiment que par la douleur, et j'aurais voulu que s'enfonçassent plus solidement encore en moi ces clous qui y rivaient sa mémoire' (II, 759). Indeed, in order to expiate his guilt Marcel imagines a kind of suicidal self-punishment in which he takes his grandmother's suffering upon himself, as she had taken his upon her: 'Ma grand'mère que j'avais, avec tant d'indifférence, vue agoniser et mourir près de moi! O puissé-je, en expiation, quand mon oeuvre serait terminée, blessé sans remède, souffrir de longues heures, abandonné de tous, avant de mourir!' (III, 902). And, of course, at the end of the novel, he imagines himself as a dying mother who spends his last, painful days ministering to the needs of his 'child,' the work of art that he has nurtured for so long.

Marcel's – that is to say, Proust's – penetrating psychological analysis parallels Freud's key text 'Mourning and Melancholia,' written about the same time, which says that grief is an ambivalent, guilt-ridden identification with the dead in which we 'incorporate' them into ourselves and then gradually, in the process of mourning, give them up again.[5] This is similar to what happens in the case of Albertine, where Marcel, falling out of love with her, loses his old identity and changes into a new self that no longer loves her. Albertine's death is, in a sense, a metaphor for Marcel's loss of her, for the fact that she no longer means anything to him, the literal event ironically confirming what is already true psychologically, just as mourning offers a specific paradigm for the broader psychological category of 'melancholia.' In the case of his grandmother's death, his double sense of loss and guilt is too great for him to acknowledge his real feelings, and only later is he able to undo his attachment to her by punishing himself for what he has done to her.

It seems clear, moreover, that Marcel's grandmother is an idealized maternal figure, even more loving and self-sacrificing than his mother, and that the 'double murder' which identifies his sadistic cruelty toward Albertine with his childish ungratefulness toward his grandmother also implies a deep sense of guilt toward his mother – briefly glimpsed in the *drame du coucher* when, 'forcing' her to spend the night with him, he feels he has let her down. The intense, suspicious, ambivalent, potentially violent relationship between Marcel and Albertine, between any two lovers in Proust's novel, seems to grow out of the uneasy dependence of a child on its mother, the overwhelming need for love, attention, and approval that, by the ordinary limitations of real life, can never be fully satisfied. The potential violence of these relationships is perhaps best illustrated by the condensed scenario of Proust's early newspaper article, 'Sentiments filiaux d'un parricide,' in which, soon after his own mother's death, he attempts to 'explain' the apparently irrational and motiveless actions of a man who kills his mother and then himself. After comparing this sensational story to classical tragedies, including *Oedipus Rex,* Proust asserts that even murder – like Mlle Vinteuil's 'sadistic' betrayal of her father – may be a distorted expression of love. According to him, the wildest, most insane acts of violence may reveal what are actually universal desires, normally subdued and hidden, a view that Freud himself had suggested a little earlier,[6] and the suffering that we cause our parents is just a slow way of killing them, little by little.

It is this sense of dangerous and disturbing feelings within him that makes Marcel say that he has 'murdered' his grandmother, the person he loves best, his mother's mother, who represents for him the epitome of maternal love. Everything, including Albertine's infidelity, reminds Marcel of his own guilt. The scene at Montjouvain, linked with Albertine, may have returned from the depths of his memory 'pour mon supplice, pour mon châtiment . . . d'avoir laissé mourir ma grand'mère' (II, 1115). The memory returns like an avenging demon, like Orestes who returns to punish his father's murderer, but Marcel has not murdered a father, he has 'murdered' a mother (his grandmother), as Orestes himself is forced to do. In short, women betray him because he has betrayed, abandoned, 'murdered' them, though the reverse may also be true. Ironically, Marcel's mother proves most faithful, it seems, not to her husband but to another woman, her own mother, Marcel's grandmother, whom he also loves as he loves her.

III

Odette is, ironically, not Swann's type, but his identification of her with Botticelli's painting of Zipporah allows him to see her in terms of an aesthetic image, to assimilate her thin, languishing, melancholy type of beauty, which would not normally please him, to his aesthetic tastes. By the same token, his association of Odette with Vinteuil's sonata enables him to substitute a kind of magical, immaterial essence – much easier to assimilate – for the flesh-and-blood woman who may disappoint him and, for that matter, betray him. Marcel, too, 'loves' the Duchesse de Guermantes because she promises to be an animated version of medieval tapestries and stained-glass windows. He first falls in love with Gilberte, even before he sees her, because she is the friend of an artist, Bergotte. Albertine as well is the embodiment of an idea, a healthy, athletic, birdlike being whose natural element is the sea – like the beautiful girl who reminds Stephen Dedalus of a seabird – or more precisely, not an idea but an image, the vague, barely differentiated outline of a birdlike creature set against the hazy background of the sea. Just as Marcel imagines loving a peasant-girl who might spring up magically from the Roussainville woods, or Mme de Stermaria whom he thinks of as the incarnation, the *genius loci,* of Brittany, he falls in love, at first, with an idea or image that is already a projection of his own imagination. One has to have a paradigm, a type, to love, and, where the woman does not fit the type, as in Odette's case, Swann performs a kind of metaphorical substitution which enables him to love Odette in the guise of Botticelli's Zipporah.

It should be noted that Swann's and Marcel's tastes are both divided between two divergent types: healthy, apple-cheeked, sensuous women, peasants or working-class girls, especially milk-maids, and pale, thin, pensive, tired-looking women, more 'aesthetic' or simply more aristocratic. The first type is wild, natural, alive, the second more refined, more 'cultivated,' a creature of the drawing-room rather than the fields or the sea, more thoughtful and less physical. Now Odette belongs to the second type though she is by no means aristocratic, and Mme de Guermantes, though she is aristocratic and might have stepped out of a stained-glass window, is also radiant and alive. Still, the basic dichotomy implies a desire for two contrary things: spontaneous, natural life, exactly what sickly, inhibited Marcel fears he doesn't possess, and the perfect, unattainable beauty which is possible only in art. Moreover, the pale, languishing, melancholy look of the second type, when it is no longer associated with 'aesthetic' or aristocratic sensibilities, when it is simply sickly and 'neurasthenic,' may be a reflection of Marcel's own self-image, presenting him with a kind of alter ego whom he might like or dislike for that very reason. The problem is that one loves what one doesn't have, what is different from oneself, but the greater the difference, the more mysterious, frightening, dangerous, and unattainable the irreducible 'other' becomes.

Marcel seems just as interested in being invited to Gilberte's house, getting to know her parents, as in winning her affection, and *Du Côté de chez Swann* ends with a paean not to her but her mother, as the incarnation of womanly beauty: 'c'est Mme Swann que je voulais voir, et j'attendais qu'elle passât, ému comme si s'avait été Gilberte' (I, 418). In the last, waning stages of his love, he winds up attending Odette's salon and avoiding Gilberte. His fondness for older women extends of course to Mme de Guermantes, who not only seems a queen, a reigning beauty, like Odette in the Bois de Boulogne, but is in fact a highborn, noble lady with the air of a sovereign. Though Odette has dubious social origins, she and her daughter Gilberte seem to Marcel impossibly above him on the social scale, and this social gap is one of the factors in his attraction to them. This 'courtly' love for a highborn lady, refined and exalted, impossible to touch, as if she were the Virgin Mary on a stained-glass window, corresponds, as we have seen, to another, more sensual desire for a lowly peasant or working girl, someone who will respond to one's advances and about whom one need have no moral scruples. As if following a rule of exogamy, Marcel (like Swann) wants someone either above him or below him, never of his own social class, where the women are too common to be idealized and not common enough to be freely exploited, as if they were his own sister or cousin. Albertine turns out to be a 'poor' orphan, like Odette whose mother 'sells' her to a rich man, though she has rich, snobbish relatives, but she and the other girls in the little band seem so 'fast,' so vulgar, so unconstrained by conventional bourgeois manners, 'd'un genre si voyou,' that Marcel takes them for 'des maîtresses de coureurs cyclistes, de champions de boxe' (I, 845).

The distinction between high and low is a distinction between chaste and willing, but the signs of these 'moral' categories prove deceptive. The contemptuous gesture that Gilberte seems to give Marcel from behind the hawthorn hedge turns out, years later, to have been a frank expression of desire, and the 'loose' behavior of Albertine and her friends seems to be belied, a little later, by her refusal to let him kiss her. The impression of a 'virtuous' Albertine is also temporary and, after proving herself willing, she turns into her opposite, an unfaithful and promiscuous Albertine. The woman's glance is the first crucial (though ambiguous) sign of her inner feelings, and Marcel first turns his attention to Albertine because she seems to notice him, to return his look, just as Gilberte arouses his interest by appearing *not* to notice him. Even Mme de Guermantes appears to bestow a glance upon Marcel in the Combray church: miraculously she waves and smiles to him in the theater, but on the street she hardly seems to know him. In short, each woman is always two women, one who is willing to know him and one who isn't, one flirtatious and one unresponsive. Once again, however, the division into opposing types is not so simple, for the cold, hostile, contemptuous look – such as Gilberte appears to give – attracts him even more than its opposite: rejection (like absence) making his heart grow fonder. Hesitating between Albertine and Andrée, he loves the one who refuses to see him. When he quarrels with two other members of the band, in a kind of paradigm of his desire for what he doesn't have, the one 'qui ferait les premiers pas me rendrait le calme, c'est l'autre que j'aimerais si elle restait brouillée' (III, 505).

Already, as a child, Marcel desperately wants his mother to stay with him, if only to calm his anxiety, but he has learned to love the 'distant' mother who is continually abandoning him, who seems indifferent to his deepest needs. In later life, a little masochistically, he repeats the process of falling in love with someone who may not love him, who is bound (it seems) to be unfaithful. As Marcel points out, 'Albertine, grosse et brune, ne ressemblait pas à Gilberte, élancée et rousse, mais pourtant elles avaient la même étoffe de santé, et dans les mêmes joues sensuelles toutes les deux un regard dont on saisissait difficilement la signification' (III, 501-2). In short, healthy and sensuous, they seem like temptresses, giving him a seductive look which he may have misread. Indeed, the members of the little band attract him not simply by their natural spontaneity, wild and a little vulgar, but by their brazen contempt for others, as when one of them leaps over an old man seated in a chair and another cries, sarcastically, 'C'pauvre vieux, i m'fait d'la peine, il a l'air à moitié crevé' (I, 792). As in the case of Gilberte's ambiguous look, it is this arrogant, scornful, pitiless, cruel, even sadistic demeanor which really seduces Marcel, a kind of 'vulgar' version of the queenly hauteur which noble ladies like Mme de Guermantes, looking down from their lofty social pinnacles, do not have to bother to show. It is the same queenly hauteur shown, on a higher social level but still potentially crude and vulgar, by M. de Charlus, playing the *grande dame*.

Marcel's exaggerated, idealized infatuation with older women that seem to tower above him on the social scale, like queens in fairy-tales, suggests a typical childish fantasy of an exalted, beautiful, noble mother, a 'family romance' of the kind described by Freud, though one which we might have expected Marcel to have long since outgrown. [7] But his desire for a sensual, seductive, slightly vulgar, socially inferior girl is the necessary counterpart to this idealization, the black-and-white logic of childish fantasy implying that all women (beginning with one's mother) are either pure, noble virgins, like the secularized Madonna played by the Duchesse de Guermantes, or promiscuous whores.[8] Social status becomes a sign of moral respectability, and it is significant that, as in the 'special type of object choice' described by Freud, Marcel falls in love with a crude, unrefined Albertine and then wants to 'uplift' her, educate her tastes in art, improve her vocabulary – and keep her virtuous. By the same token, the second Proustian type turns out to be, in the extreme case, a prostitute: Odette is a courtesan, Rachel a working girl who works in a brothel. The two girls recommended by Saint-Loup, the young 'prostitute' of a good family and Baroness Putbus's ready-and-willing maid, both represent complex fusions of the initial whore/'lady' dichotomy, the first because she is a 'lady' and the second because she works for one, like the servants 'qui disent "nous" en parlant des duchesses' (II, 723). The girl passing in front of his house, whom Marcel, misconstruing her name, mistakes for the prostitute from a good family, turns out to be Gilberte.

In the bizarre, Dostoyevskian interlude following Albertine's departure, to console himself in his grief, Marcel picks up a poor girl on the street, invites her home, dandles her on his knee, and sends her away again after paying her off with a five-hundred franc note. He is surprised when the girl's parents, outraged, return the money and call the police, as if the five-hundred francs should absolve him of any wrongdoing. From Gilberte and the girls of the little band to the 'poor little girl' on the street and Gilberte's teenage daughter, Marcel exhibits a preference for young girls, sometimes very young, though he claims that it is not he but the head of the Sûreté (who admonishes him) who has a weakness for little girls! We know that he also likes older women, Mme de Guermantes and Mme Swann, who seem to be idealized, romanticized versions of his mother, pure and noble creatures, almost goddesses, while the young girls, especially if they come from a lower social class, are coarse, physical, down-to-earth, and more obviously sexual. These girls are ambiguously virginal and seductive at the same time, probably because they are too young to have lost their virginity, and this is a major source of their attraction. Indeed, the contradictions and dichotomies of Marcel's desires – the split between exalted mother-figures and 'working girls' who work in brothels, the ambiguity of innocent, virginal temptresses – suggest a deep uneasiness about female sexuality, a need to believe that women (especially mothers) are pure and virginal accompanied by a disturbing fear that they are not. This fear is also a wish, a natural result of his own sexual desires, supported by Bloch's assurances that all women are ready and willing to make love, but the idea of his own mother's sexuality is a dangerous, guilt-inspiring conception, which may lead to a fear and mistrust of women, a feeling that they are all cruel temptresses (*femmes fatales*) waiting to betray him.

Marcel's collective love for the different members of the little band, his uncertainty about which of them to love, the sense that they are inseparable and indistinguishable, leads to a variety of possible interpretations. In the first place, Marcel loves a type, a preconceived image, not a specific individual, and the various different girls illustrate, like an allegorical tableau, the changing faces of Albertine, different and yet finally alike. This protean, changeable quality reflects the overflowing, spontaneous 'life' that Marcel would like to capture but can't. Moreover, the difficulty of distinguishing between the different girls stems from the underdeveloped, childlike appearance of their faces, made clear by a photograph of them taken just a few years earlier: now they are just beyond puberty, 'à peine mais déjà sorties d'un âge où on change si complétement,' but then 'ces enfants trop jeunes étaient encore à ce degré élémentaire de formation où la personnalité n'a pas mis son sceau sur chaque visage' (I,823). This childlike quality appeals to Marcel because of its prepubescent innocence as well as its laughing, joyful exuberance – something which he, prematurely old and melancholy like his aunt Léonie, can only envy – but it also contributes to that essential narcissistic attraction to the child he once was and in a sense always will be, the child whom he loves as his mother loves him. These prepubescent children with their indeterminate features could almost as well have been boys instead of girls. Clinging to this early, innocent, childlike or at least adolescent self-image, Marcel retains his preference for young girls even after he himself has grown old, as if hoping (in the case of Gilberte's daughter) that they could restore his own youth.

The attraction which Albertine seems to inspire in *other* girls – 'Dès son enfance, Albertine avait toujours eu en admiration devant elle quatre ou cinq petites camarades' (I, 935), which may have been the origin of the little band – may inspire a similar attraction in Marcel, but there is a sense in which he, like just another member of the band, loves only an alternate version of himself, that all these vague attractions are childish, not clearly heterosexual (to the extent that they are sexual at all), and fundamentally narcissistic. Indeed, the 'sisterly' affection of the little band may inspire a brotherly affection in Marcel, innocent and yet disturbingly incestuous, the love of one barely differentiated 'spore' for another in a primitive attempt (so it would seem) to fuse and recreate the original, collective unity of the 'madrepore,' the 'mother' structure out of which these siblings are created. For it is precisely the analogy to 'ces organismes primitifs où l'individu n'existe guère par lui-même, est plutôt constitué par le polypier que par chacun des polypes qui le composent' (I, 823), that best explains Marcel's attraction to the little band: it enables him to conceive of love as the union of barely differentiated individuals, the reunion of a child and its mother, where the ordinary distinctions between brothers and sisters, children and parents, oneself and others, no longer apply. The little band may be a primitive, prototypical social microcosm, a self-contained social group with manners and customs of its own, separated from the rest of society but appearing homogeneous to those outside it, a collective unity which Marcel imagines as a kind of amorphous mother-organism that he would like to be assimilated into.

IV

The confusion of sexual identity appears, of course, in Charlus, who 'hates' young men for their effeminacy yet seems to have a delicate, 'feminine' sensibility of his own, who has a reputation as a womanizer (he is rumored in Combray circles to have been Odette's lover), and whose penetrating, disdainful stares make Marcel think he is a thief, a spy, or a madman. Charlus may claim to dislike effeminacy because he himself is effeminate, because he really does prefer strong, 'virile' men, but also because, contrary to appearances, despite his devotion to his dead wife's memory, he dislikes and fears women. He can be violent and abusive toward the young men who attract him, if he doesn't get his way, but he also abuses women he considers social upstarts. Charlus's brutal, arrogant rages supposedly conceal a gentle, kind, sensitive nature, as if he 'took after' some female relative, as if the real Charlus hidden beneath his haughty exterior were a woman:

> car ce à quoi me faisait penser cet homme, qui était si épris, qui se piquait si fort de virilité, à qui tout le monde semblait odieusement efféminé, ce à quoi il me faisait penser tout d'un coup, tant il en avait passagèrement les traits, l'expression, le sourire, c'était à une femme (II, 604).

needed in the past. The theme of homosexuality is significant in the novel not simply because Proust was a homosexual but because it provides an extreme case of the underlying contradictions and ambivalences of love. The love of men for other men who are *not* homosexuals – a narcissistic desire, paradoxically, for the 'manliness' they don't possess – also confirms Marcel's rule that we love those who don't love us, loving them all the more for that reason.

The idea of roles is ambiguous because each lover plays more than one role, even at any one time, but it does reflect Proust's belief that life follows a limited number of patterns, that the parts we play are preconceived, prearranged. Changeable, histrionic, melodramatic, hiding his 'true' self but overplaying his part, becoming a parody of himself, Charlus is clearly a 'theatrical' character, always performing. His first meeting with Jupien turns into a charade or pantomime, and, in Jupien's brothel, trying to convince himself of the reality of the scene he is playing, he complains that the man who is beating him isn't brutal enough, isn't a criminal, is only acting. Besides, he wears makeup to look younger and in the end he appears as an old, enfeebled King Lear. Proust uses theatrical metaphors to underscore the effects of time, to show that each person is many, successive selves, but acting and disguise are specifically connected with sexual ambiguity: as in the portrait of 'Miss Sacripant,' whose costume implies that she is an actress dressed for a part or else a transvestite, unless she is dressed for the part of a transvestite, like one of Shakespeare's boy actors playing girls disguised as boys. Odette herself plays many parts in her life, and as the mysterious lady in pink she appears to Marcel as a kind of actress, *cocottes* not being clearly distinguished from actresses in his mind. Rachel, an actress, begins her career as a prostitute, as if the former were only one step removed from the latter. The actress Léa has a notorious reputation as a (promiscuous) homosexual, and the rival who had been walking with Gilberte along the Champs-Elysées turns out to have been Léa dressed like a man, another ambiguous 'Miss Sacripant.'

The made-up, red-cheeked dancer that Rachel flirts with, in the theater, 'un jeune homme en toque de velours noir, en jupe hortensia, les joues crayonnées de rouge' (II, 177), seems to be the consummate performer, a 'madman' who leaves his everyday self behind and acts out an ecstatic dream, a childlike 'narcissist' who loves to perform and to be admired for his performance, going so far

as to mimic, to parody himself (like a *pasticheur*). Rachel suggests
that only a man could use his hands the way the dancer does, as if
he would fondle a woman in the same way, but then, contradicting
herself, she says he looks like a woman and imagines a curious
ménage-à-trois with him and a girlfriend of hers. In short, the dancer's
narcissistic pleasure in his own movements is ambiguously, childish-
ly erotic, and, painted, costumed, dressed in a skirt, he seems to be
playing an equivocal, androgynous role. Saint-Loup, jealous of
Rachel's flirtation, vents his anger by punching a journalist and
then, moments later, a man who propositions him, a strange and
implausible sequence of events which we might take to imply that
he is jealous not of Rachel but of the dancer, who is flirting with
Rachel instead of himself. Actresses like Rachel, Léa and 'Miss
Sacripant' are sexually dissolute, even sexually ambiguous – as if the
idea of playing a role and putting on a costume meant playing the
part of a transvestite and putting on the clothes of the opposite
sex – not because Proust shares the old puritanical view of the
theater but because he recognizes the narcissistic element in acting
and the theatrical element in love.

Needless to say, however, 'Marcel' is not Proust and we are not
reading the story of Proust's life: Marcel is always the observer, the
voyeur, imagining scenes in which he is betrayed by others, 'writing'
the scenario for new 'primal' scenes in which the woman he loves
betrays him with another woman. Why then is this betrayal, unlike
its oedipal prototype, homosexual? Why is he obsessed not simply
by Albertine's unfaithfulness but by her homosexuality? Two
contradictory answers suggest themselves: either Proust is projecting
his own unacknowledged homosexuality onto Albertine, Marcel's
obsessive anxiety reflecting his own displaced guilt, or else he is
projecting his heterosexual desires, his love of women, onto her,
providing her with the kind of lovers he himself would like to have.
Marcel's almost fawning admiration for Saint-Loup, his desperate
desire to win his friendship, even before he meets him, culminating
in the blissful night he spends not in some strange hotel room but in
Saint-Loup's room in the garrison at Doncières, suggests something
more than friendship. His prurient, voyeuristic interest in Charlus's
secret life is also suspect. On the other hand, as if identifying himself
with Albertine and trying to see through her eyes, he begins to desire
the women she herself has had affairs with, including Andrée,
Albertine's 'sister' in the little band, although he once thought her

too 'neurasthenic,' too much like himself. Does this mean that he shares Albertine's homosexual tastes or that she shares his attraction to women? Or, for that matter, should we violate the integrity of the text and imagine Albertine as a male Albert or Alfred (Agostinelli) whose girlfriends are 'really' girlfriends?[10] Marcel suspects Saint-Loup of having seduced Albertine but his jealousy quickly subsides, not because he doesn't love Albertine, nor simply because he fears only women, but because he may also 'love' Saint-Loup.

Of course, as many impatient readers will have long since concluded, there is no solution, in the text, to these dizzying vortices of identification, projection, and displacement,[11] except the realization that it is precisely sexual ambiguity that appeals to Proust, satisfying both the narcissism and the ambivalent fear and envy of women that seem to characterize his alter ego Marcel. The issue is not homosexuality but the complex, contradictory motives that underlie any sort of love. For this reason the typical, paradigmatic object of Proustian love might be 'Miss Sacripant,' actress or transvestite, who, for that matter, doesn't really exist except in Elstir's painting and, perhaps, in Elstir's imagination. Moreover, this typical figure becomes the object not only of love but of ambivalent jealousy, a rival, the third member of a romantic triangle, the ambiguous part played by Léa, the homosexual actress, when, dressed in male clothes and walking with Gilberte, she is mistaken by Marcel for a young man. Or again, a friend quarrels with Marcel in a dream and, interpreting the dream, he takes this young man for Gilberte. According to this sexual uncertainty principle, the prototypical Proustian lover, Marcel's secret alter ego, might be Morel, the selfish, amoral, unfaithful lover of both men and women, social climber and artist, who mocks his 'fatherly' mentor Charlus, longs to 'deflower' virgins and then abandon them, loves art more than money and loves himself more than any-one else.

Morel is a central figure in Proust's 'structures of kinship' because, as a social climber and artist, heterosexual and homosexual, he plays so many contradictory roles, a kind of protean trickster whose only true love is himself. The names Morel and Marcel – like the names Charlie (Morel), Charlus, and Charles (Swann) – suggest a secret kinship, and as an artist, Morel is not only a violinist but (like Marcel) a budding writer whose articles imitate Bergotte's speaking style (not his writing) in the manner of a Proustian pastiche. Besides,

he is the son of Marcel's uncle's valet, and in his social climbing he
treats Marcel as his equal, as if he were simply a cynical, unromantic
Marcel without childish illusions, like one of those self-willed,
pseudo-revolutionary, nineteenth-century heroes who seek not to
overthrow society but to place themselves at the top of it. Morel is
ashamed of his servant father and proud of his father's 'master,'
Marcel's uncle Adolphe, who (with his romantic liaisons) hovers in
the background as a strong, sexual father-figure to both Morel and
Marcel.

In her intimate, impassioned letter to Morel, in which she
addresses him as a woman, Léa insists that he is 'so' ('en être'),
meaning not that he is homosexual but that he loves women in the
same sense as she loves women. Charlus, who opens the letter by
mistake, is bewildered by this totally ambiguous use of the term: 'ce
double mystère, où il y avait à la fois de l'agrandissement de sa
jalousie et de l'insuffisance soudaine d'une définition' (III, 215). This
peculiar relation between homosexuals of the opposite sex is either
the perfect paradigm or the *reductio ad absurdum* of Proust's uncertainty principle, but Marcel gives it a special place in his structural
analysis of homosexuality:

> Car dans les rapports qu'ils ont avec elles, ils jouent pour la
> femme qui aime les femmes le rôle d'une autre femme, et la
> femme leur offre en même temps à peu près ce qu'ils trouvent
> chez l'homme, si bien que l'ami jaloux souffre de sentir celui qu'il
> aime rivé à celle qui est pour lui presque un homme, en même
> temps qu'il le sent presque lui échapper, parce que, pour ces
> femmes, il est quelque chose qu'il ne connaît pas, une espèce de
> femme (II, 622-3).

As in any case of love between a man and a woman, each person
loves an imaginary facsimile of the other, and the other person is
only one point in a symbolic structure of possible relationships, in a
floating romantic triangle which may have even more than three
sides. According to Andrée, Morel used to procure little girls for
Albertine, initiating them into sexual relations and then, when their
moral scruples had become sufficiently weak, handing them over to
her, as if he took pleasure in what Marcel seems to fear most, the
promiscuous relations of women with other women. He brings one
of these girls to a *maison de femmes*, 'où quatre ou cinq la prirent

ensemble ou successivement. C'était sa passion, comme c'était aussi celle d'Albertine' (III, 600). He likes to 'debauch' women, to rob them of their virtue and magically transform them into whores, but, better still, he likes to watch them debauching each other, they playing the part of whores (without benefit of male clients) while he plays the procurer, the Sade-like whoremaster. Wouldn't Marcel, for all his jealousy, like to do the same: that is, does Proust attribute to Morel desires which would seem too perverse in his 'hero'?

V

Mme Verdurin's favorite game is to play the go-between for her favorites, making matches and breaking them when one of the principals (such as Swann) falls out of her favor. Like the mistress of the public toilet in the Champs-Elysées, she has a fondness for young men: since women seem less likely to remain loyal, she expels most of them from the ranks of the faithful and surrounds herself with a collection of male admirers. And it is she (not her husband) who presides over the little clan, who is the mistress, the *patronne*: the clan, like all salons, is matriarchal, and she does not care if the members are faithful to each other as long as they remain faithful to her. As the matriarch of the clan, she watches over her brood of children, marries off her 'daughters,' but expects her 'sons-in-law' to leave their clans and join hers, to follow a kind of matrilocal rule. In Proust's novel every love affair demands a third party, a go-between or rival, who often emerges as a new object of love, and in this case the third party is a 'mother-in-law,' the actual or figurative mother of the woman one loves. Swann longs to present his wife and child to the Duchesse de Guermantes, in order to win her seal of social approval, and Marcel seeks Odette's approval for his relations with Gilberte. Marcel and Albertine become members of Mme Verdurin's little clan, repeating the history of Swann and Odette. Fearing that history may repeat itself too well, Marcel worries that Albertine is going to meet her suspected lovers, Mlle Vinteuil and her friend, at the Verdurins', and in fact Mme Verdurin has arranged for Albertine to meet a potential husband, her nephew. Perhaps it should not surprise us that when, one day in Paris, Marcel decides to run through the streets after a woman, she turns out to be Mme Verdurin, whom he had been scrupulously avoiding, as if he could possibly find her desirable. In Swann's dream at the end of 'Un Amour de Swann,' Odette goes off while he ('faithful' despite himself) stays with Mme Verdurin, and, to top it off, the *patronne's* face changes shape, her nose grows longer, and she sprouts a big moustache, like the brothel-keeper Bella Cohen in Joyce's *Ulysses,* who turns into a mean and sadistic Bello. In short, the mistress is master in her own house, the social world is as matriarchal as, say, aunt Léonie's regime in Combray, and under the authority of this stern, masculine 'mother,' who adopts the father's powers as her own, everyone else is just a child.

Feeling excluded from his mother's dinner party, Marcel writes a note asking her to come upstairs and delivers it by way of Françoise, whom he says he loves because she is playing the part of a go-between for him. But the note itself is a kind of go-between, a way of reaching the other person, and letters play an increasingly important, dramatic role in Proust's novel. Swann writes a falsely accusatory letter to Odette, she writes a falsely conciliatory one from the Maison Dorée; he intercepts her letter to Forcheville, an anonymous letter informs him of her infidelities. Charlus reads Léa's letter to Morel, which gives him the confusing information that Morel is 'like that' too, and he himself writes violent letters to Morel, a 'false' one about a duel and a 'true' one threatening to murder him. Marcel longs for a letter from Gilberte, writes one appealing to her father Swann, writes another to her, pretending to break off their relationship. In the same way he writes a 'Dear Albertine' letter taking back the yacht and the Rolls he has bought for her. He writes a telegram begging her to return, her aunt wires him news of her death, and he receives two last, 'posthumous' letters from her, expressing contradictory sentiments. All these letters are attempts to communicate but also to deceive and manipulate; they do not tell the simple truth, not just because someone is lying but because messages are open to misinterpretation, because communication is never simple. In Venice Marcel receives a telegram from Albertine protesting that she is still alive, a message that seems to come from beyond the grave, but a later letter from Gilberte makes him realize that the clerk had misread the message, that the signature *Albertine* should have read *Gilberte,* her *G* resembling an *A.* 'On devine en lisant, on crée,' says Marcel, adding: 'et ce n'est pas seulement dans la lecture des lettres et des télégrammes, pas seulement dans toute lecture' (III, 656), as if our attempt to interpret real-life situations were also a kind of reading, a process of deciphering which is not always successful.[12]

These misleading, ambiguous messages have to be read between the lines, but one can also, in a sense, convey a message through *another* person's words, as when Gilberte gives Marcel a copy of Bergotte's pamphlet on Racine. Is it Racine or Bergotte or simply Gilberte that Marcel is interested in? Books are one of the favorite gifts exchanged by Proust's characters: Charlus also gives Marcel one of Bergotte's books, before demanding it back, and Marcel's grandmother gives him a present of four novels by George Sand. It is as if, through the book, these characters might be able to share an aesthetic pleasure, and both his grandmother and Swann give Marcel reproductions of paintings (Swann gives him Giotto's *Virtues and Vices*). Indeed, gifts seem to play an important, symbolic, almost magical role in Proust's novel, as they do in the 'primitive' societies described in Marcel Mauss's essay on *The Gift*.[13] For example, in addition to Bergotte's pamphlet, Gilberte gives Marcel a marble the same color as her eyes. When Swann (accidentally) forgets his cigarette case at Odette's house, she writes to him, 'Que n'y avez-vous oublié aussi votre coeur, je ne vous aurais pas laissé le reprendre' (I, 222), as if one's 'heart,' one's love, could literally be given to someone else. In the case of the pamphlet on Racine, Marcel feels that he possesses something not only of Gilberte but of the author Bergotte: though he treasures the pamphlet because Gilberte gave it to him, he first became interested in Gilberte because she was a friend of Bergotte. Like her parents, Bergotte presides over the first stage of their love like a spiritual, aesthetic 'godfather,' the attendant 'genius' of beauty and art.

Like the 'mother-in-law' who marries off her daughters, this artist 'father-in-law' plays a key role in the love affairs of Proust's novel. Marcel admires Elstir for his painting, but he becomes another go-between, the man who can introduce him to Albertine, as if he were (in Marcel's eyes) the spiritual father of the orphan girl. In a sense, in loving any daughter, Marcel embraces also the mother (Odette), the 'sisters' like Andrée and the other members of the little band, the artist 'father' who raises their love above the merely physical, merely naturalistic, level. Marcel embraces a whole family, recreating one to replace the one he has to leave behind, creating a 'family romance' in which the new mother is rich and beautiful and the new father is a brilliant artist. Vinteuil, the third major artist-figure in the novel, presides over the love of his daughter and her friend in an ironic variation upon this same pattern. If we put Albertine in Mlle Vinteuil's place, as Marcel does, then we see that all three artists are symbolic, 'totemistic' 'fathers-in-law' (as well as fathers) to Marcel. In another variation, the actress Berma, a fourth

Table 3.1   Major 'kinship' relations in Proust's *Recherche*

'son' (or daughter)	go-between	wife, mistress, or lover	'mother-in-law'	'father-in-law'	homo-sexual rival
Marcel	(parents-in-law)	Gilberte	Odette	Swann Bergotte	Léa
Swann	(parents-in-law)	Odette	Mme Verdurin	Charlus, Botticelli	
Marcel	Françoise	Marcel's mother	(Marcel's grandmother)	Swann, Marcel's father	
Marcel	Gilberte	Mlle de Saint-Loup	Gilberte	Saint-Loup (Charlus?)	
Marcel	Saint-Loup	Mme de Guermantes			
Marcel	Elstir	Albertine (cousin or sister)	Mme Bontemps (aunt)	Elstir	Andrée, Léa, etc.
(Marcel)		Mlle Vinteuil		M. Vinteuil	Mlle Vinteuil's friend
Marcel	(Elstir)	'Miss Sacripant' (Odette)		Elstir	
Marcel	Morel's father (valet)	lady in pink (Odette)		uncle Adolphe	
Morel		Jupien's niece		Charlus, Jupien	
Saint-Loup	Marcel?	Gilberte	Odette		
Gilberte	Marcel?	Saint-Loup	Mme de Guermantes (aunt)	Charlus (uncle)	
Charlus	Marcel?	Morel	Mme Verdurin		(Léa)
Saint-Loup	Marcel?	Rachel	madam of brothel	Halévy ('Rachel when from the Lord')	Léa, (male dancer)
young Cambremer	Charlus	Jupien's niece		Jupien, Charlus	
Jupien's niece	Charlus	young Cambremer	Mme de Cambremer	M. de Cambremer, Legrandin (uncle)	Charlus

artist-figure, is betrayed and abandoned by her daughter and son-in-law – for another actress, another 'artist,' Rachel.

Proust, whose characters seem so interested in the genealogies of old noble families, creates symbolic structures of 'kinship' which seem to take precedence over actual family ties (see Table 3.1). As Marcel himself says: 'De relations qui ne sont pas consacrées par les lois découlent des liens de parenté aussi multiples, aussi complexes, plus solides seulement, que ceux qui naissent du mariage' (III, 262). Marcel likes to have a 'sisterly' Albertine, innocent, affectionate, and domestic, to comfort him for the cruel betrayals of the other Albertine, and he pretends to the Verdurins that she is his cousin. This imaginary kinship implies that he wants someone to share his house and minister to his needs, a 'wife' as well as a mistress, a 'mother' as well as a wife, but also that his love recreates earlier, even incestuous family bonds. Proust underscores the protean, equivocal, friend-or-enemy role of the 'third party,' like that of the *other* parent in the oedipal triangle, and he also shows us that the third party is often a surrogate parent. Swann uses Charlus to keep an eye on Odette, like a eunuch in a harem, which makes people suspect that Charlus is Odette's lover although he is really Swann's equivocal 'friend.' Marcel wants Saint-Loup to introduce him to his aunt, the Duchesse de Guermantes, to use him as a go-between, as he later sends him to bribe Albertine's aunt and engineer Albertine's return, but Marcel also 'loves' him as a friend, as he loves that other go-between Françoise.

Morel seduces and abandons Jupien's niece, after calling her a whore, and Charlus – who has taken a fatherly interest in their relationship, who would like to play the role of 'father-in-law' in order to make Morel (and perhaps also Jupien) more dependent on him – winds up playing the part of her patron, adopting her, and arranging her marriage to the young Marquis de Cambremer, who shares his own sexual preferences. Dying of typhoid a few weeks after the wedding, she seems merely a pawn in the homosexual relations of her 'father' Charlus and Morel, of Charlus and her uncle Jupien, an item of exchange (a gift) whereby the 'father' gives away his daughter in exchange for the sexual favors of his future 'son-in-law.' Odette's mother is reputed to have sold her to a wealthy Englishman, but if 'love' can be bought and sold, Jupien's niece becomes nothing other than an object of exchange herself, traded by men not for money but for another kind of love.[14]

These false bonds of 'kinship' imply that love is a commercial transaction, a more subtle form of prostitution, but Marcel's interest in the symbolic 'mothers' and 'fathers' of his girlfriends – the queens and artist-kings of his family romance – suggests that family ties, true bonds of kinship, mean more to him than relations that are purely sexual, which are also more dangerous. He wishes not only to find a woman whom he can love like his mother or a girl whom he can love like himself, as his mother loved him, but also to join a social group – an extended family – from which he feels himself excluded, whether it be Gilberte's family (the house of Swann), the little band of precocious, 'orphaned' sisters at Balbec, or the Faubourg Saint-Germain itself. But if no social group can fulfill his child-centered fantasies of family life, then he must turn his back on 'society' and seek a more subtle kind of fulfillment within himself.[15] Instead of venerating artists as totemistic fathers, he must become an artist himself.

4 Proust, Joyce, and the metaphor of flowers

Both Proust and Joyce explore the ambiguities of sexual relations, make jealousy a condition of friendship and love, imply (in Joyce's words) that *amor matris* may be the only true thing in life, investigate 'mourning and melancholia,' associate death with the transcendence of art, try to stop time or reverse it or escape it, try to solve the riddle of male/female differences, blur the distinction between inner and outer worlds, pretend to believe in magical substances or essences, and invent their own myths of artistic creation or 'procreation.' The differences between Joyce and Proust – in the treatment of homosexuality, in Joyce's emphasis on fathers in addition to mothers – are revealing and significant, but their complex, dialectical awareness of the relation between art and life, between inner and outer worlds, sets them apart from many other writers, even many of their fellow modernists. Indeed, the surprisingly close parallels between Proust's and Joyce's texts – between their metaphorical strategies – deserve special attention. This chapter, though it may seem digressive, is an attempt to read Proust in the light of comparative 'evidence' which is particularly illuminating and which, I feel, should not be ignored.

A l'Ombre des jeunes filles en fleurs, the title of the second volume of Proust's *Recherche,* turns flowers into a metaphor for the incipient, emerging, budding sexuality of adolescent girls, but this association is already implied by the 'real' flowers, the pink and white hawthorns, of Combray, which move the young Marcel by their visual beauty. Marcel associates the festal flowers with celebrations of the Virgin Mary – 'dans sa fraîche toilette rose l'arbuste catholique et délicieux' (I, 140) – and just as he imagines the blossoming of the flowers in church as the careless, spontaneous movement of 'une blanche jeune fille' (I, 112), so too he identifies the pink hawthorn with the little girl (Gilberte), with reddish hair and pink freckles, whom he sees behind the hedge. Gilberte's mother Odette, who appears as 'une dame en blanc' (I, 141), is actually the same mysterious 'dame en rose,' either an actress or a courtesan, whom Marcel has met at his uncle Adolphe's. The color of the hawthorns is, like the color associated with the women, ambiguous, variable, and deceptive. In fact, the pale buds of the hawthorn, when they open, disclose 'de rouges sanguines' and betray, 'plus encore que les fleurs, l'essence particulière, irrésistible, de l'épine' (I, 140).

The opposition between pink and innocent white,[1] the association with the Virgin Mary, with young girls, and with a lady who isn't an innocent young girl, the particular emphasis on blossoming, the opening of buds into mature and beautiful flowers, the glimpse of the girl behind the hedge, through an arch of pink flowers, and the crucial exposure of a blood-red splash of color on the inside of pale buds, all imply an underlying preoccupation with the mysteries of virginity and sex: with the loss of virginity in intercourse (the blood-red stain caused by 'deflowering'), with the disillusioning metamorphosis of an innocent virgin into a not-so-innocent lady (her mother!), with the equally mysterious metamorphosis of a girl 'blossoming' into a sexually mature woman (marked, on the most literal level, by the blood-red stain of menstruation), or simply with the mysterious, frightening, barely glimpsed sight of a girl's genitals, which seems to disclose (in the fantasy of a boy familiar with his own anatomy) a blood-red wound. In short, the pink hawthorns, white flowers tinged red, are reassuringly innocent and yet ambiguously seductive at the same time, like the young, pubescent girls *en fleurs* who will be Marcel's special province in love.

The *jeunes filles en fleurs* of Balbec, spontaneous, youthful, alive, unselfconsciously natural, like seagulls or flowers, are adolescent girls on the verge of sexual maturity, their frank, uninhibited manners less sexual than tomboyish. In fact, these athletic, tomboyish girls – the cyclist Albertine who plays golf and 'ferret' and wears a polo cap, the girl who plays leapfrog with the old gentleman, as well as the Gilberte who plays prisoner's base – may remind Marcel of his own boyish, adolescent self. This narcissistic desire for someone like himself reduces (but does not eliminate) the mysterious and alien 'otherness' of the other person, helping him to close the gap between himself and the unpossessible person that he loves. In many ways, however, these healthy, tomboyish girls are the exact opposites of sickly, nervous, overly mannered, possibly even effeminate(?) Marcel, representing for him the self-sustaining 'life' that he both lacks and desires. In fact, 'life' seems to be a magical quality that the *other* person always possesses, the mysterious essence of the life that person leads when one is not around, the evanescent, insubstantial quality that one tries to possess for oneself. Ironically, Marcel takes Andrée for a 'créature saine et primitive' like the rest of the band, but she turns out to be 'trop intellectuelle, trop nerveuse, trop maladive, trop semblable à moi' (I, 943). The narcissistic element in love has to contend with the desire to possess what one doesn't have, the attraction for one's opposite.

The confusion about the appearance, the identity, even the sex of the person one loves – the ambiguous, transitional condition of *jeunes filles en fleurs* – is illustrated by Elstir's remarkable portrait of 'Miss Sacripant,' who turns out to be Odette in her pre-Swann days. With short hair, a cap like a bowler hat, and a cigarette in her hand, the model seems to be an actress 'en demi-travesti,' and her appearance is so ambiguous that she seems to be first 'une fille un peu garçonnière' and then 'un jeune efféminé vicieux et songeur' (I, 848-9). Marcel likens the meeting of two homosexuals to the pollination of a flower by a bee, as if the flower represented the 'female' side of the relation, but the literal token of virginity represented by the flower (of the *jeunes filles en fleurs*) is itself sexually ambiguous, an imaginary, 'poeticized,' feminized phallus – in Freudian terms, a fetish – which might suggest that young girls are not so different from boys after all.[2] Marcel may like to think of mothers as pure and virginal, but the metamorphosis of an innocent girl into a sexually mature woman frightens him. The fantasy that sexual 'flowering' is not incompatible with possessing a 'flower' reassures him: he makes a fetish of virginity, of sexual innocence, as if women lost their quasi-phallic 'flowers' in sexual intercourse and only then became an alien species, the opposite sex. When Albertine grants him the favors she had previously denied, he wonders if someone has in the interim 'robbed' her of her 'virtue,' of her virginity, and thereby transferred her from the category of girls who don't to the category of girls who do. In this case he prefers the second category, but there is a suggestion that he would like *someone else* to have the first sexual relations, to perform the initiatory rite, as if 'stealing' a girl's virginity might have dangerous consequences for oneself.

Moreover, in one remarkable description of Albertine's naked body, Marcel abandons the fetishistic pretense that a woman's body is like a flower – except for Albertine's breasts, which seem like two pieces of fruit – and reveals that he prefers the smooth, closed junction of a woman's thighs to the 'ugly' appendage that disfigures a man's anatomy: 'la place qui chez l'homme s'enlaidit comme du crampon resté fiché dans une statue descellée' (III, 79). Instead of implying that girls – with their 'flowers' – are like boys after all, he seems to wish that men (including himself) looked like women, without the disfiguring appendage. Either way, he would like to eliminate the essential difference between male and female anatomy, and although Albertine is naked, her belly is described as *hiding* the crucial spot between her thighs. There is no opening, only a reassuringly closed curve: 'son ventre . . . se refermait, à la jonction des cuisses, par deux valves d'une courbe aussi assoupie, aussi reposante, aussi claustrale que celle de l'horizon quand le soleil a disparu' (III, 79).

For Joyce's Stephen Dedalus, as for Proust's hero Marcel, the ideal object of love is a kind of virgin temptress who appears ambiguously innocent and seductive at the same time. Marcel can't tell whether Gilberte and Albertine, with their equivocal looks, gestures, and responses, are 'virtuous' or not, but the uncertainty appeals to him. Stephen thinks that the girl on the tram, Emma, is trying to seduce him, and ten years later she becomes the 'temptress' of his villanelle. Even as temptress, however, she is the object of praise and homage, as if he were simply adapting a hymn to the Virgin Mary. The birdlike girl on the beach – the identical image in which Albertine first appears to Marcel – makes a mute appeal to him, without shame, as Gilberte may have been doing from behind the hawthorn hedge, but she is innocent and childlike, beautiful rather than sexual, something to see rather than touch. The flirtatious, nymphomaniacal, vain, narcissistic, and essentially infantile character Issy in *Finnegans Wake* is an exaggerated, caricatured version of these virginal temptresses, of Gerty MacDowell in *Ulysses,* a Lolita-like nymphet who seems to be two and twelve and twenty-two years old at the same time. In fact, Issy and her seven or twenty-eight alter egos, the *flower-girls,* bear a remarkable resemblance to Marcel's *jeunes filles en fleurs.* In both cases, the girls' childlike innocence is reassuring, promising harmless childhood games like 'ferret' or dancing around the maypole in place of the dangerous sexual complications of an experienced *femme fatale.*

In Joyce's work as in Proust's the image of flowers is closely

associated with the sexuality of women. The last two pages of
Molly's monologue in *Ulysses* are strewn with references to flowers:
she says she loves flowers, would like to see the place swimming in
roses, remembers Bloom (in their famous rendezvous on the hill of
Howth) calling her a flower of the mountain, tries to decide (playing
upon the first line of a song) 'shall I wear a white rose . . . or shall I
wear a red,' and agrees with Bloom that a woman's body is like a
flower (U 781-3).[3] Moreover, the swimming roses seem to be
associated with the Bay of Gibraltar at sunset, 'the sea crimson
sometimes like fire,' and the crimson sea with 'that awful deepdown
torrent,' the bloody menstrual flow 'pouring out' of Molly 'like the
sea' (U 769). Bloom speculates that Martha has a headache because
she has 'her roses' (U 79), and in his notes for *Ulysses* Joyce confirms
the identification 'rose – menses.'[4] But Bloom, playing upon the
floral connotations of his name, signs his love letters to Martha
'Henry Flower,' which makes us question whether flowers are
exclusively feminine. At the end of the 'Lotus-Eaters' chapter,
Bloom imagines his penis as 'a languid floating flower' (U 86) on
the surface of the bath-water. The implication seems to be that
swimming menstrual flowers are fetishistic substitutes for a missing
phallus, like the drawers Bloom carries around in his pocket (U 746)
or the pin that 'Mary' uses to keep her own drawers up: 'O, Mary
lost the pin of her drawers/She didn't know what to do/To keep it
up/To keep it up' (U 78). *It,* not them, as if she were keeping her
phallic pin up: there are many jokes in *Ulysses* about keeping it up,
from 'U.p.: Up' to 'who's getting it up.' Bloom's thoughts about the
pins in women's clothing lead him to reflect that there are 'No roses
without thorns' (U 78), as if a woman's body were protected by
sharp, prickly spikes, as if the menstrual 'roses' themselves were
thorny and phallic.

In the first variant of the prankquean take, in *Finnegans Wake,* just
before the prankquean urinates on the door of Jarl van Hoother's
castle, she 'pulled a rosy one' (FW 21), as if pulling a rabbit out of a
hat or picking a card out of a deck (in the third variant, she 'picked
a blank'). The context of sexual references in the story, the fact that
she is just about to urinate ('made her wit'), lead us to imagine that
there is a rose growing out of her vagina, and in the second variant
she 'nipped a paly one' (FW 22), as if nipping a flower in the bud.
Like Molly who wonders whether she should wear a white rose or a
red one, the prankquean has a pale or rosy flower in her bag of tricks

(pranks), a magical token of potency as well as virginity, and she pulls it out in order to show it to the Jarl. If she can pull it out, she can also cut it off, nipping it like a flower: this is just one more magic trick for her – it grows back again – but for the Jarl it represents the dangerous, frightening possibility that the fantasy of a female 'flower' can help to ward off. The rosy/pale dichotomy suggests a contrast between menstruation and micturition, but any fluid that comes out of a woman's body seems to become a fertile, magically powerful substance, a kind of inflammatory 'firewater' which enables the prankquean not only to set the hills on fire but also to inflame the Jarl's passions.

The pink and white hawthorns of Combray are Proust's version of Joyce's red and white roses, and it is the pink flowers, the pink freckles on Gilberte's face, the lady in pink herself, that are especially seductive. The 'rouges sanguines' on the inside of the hawthorn buds suggest what one will find when one cuts off the flower: the imaginary flower of *jeunes filles en fleurs* only hides the possibility of a bloody wound, as if the fact that girls don't have penises meant that they had lost what they had once had. The blood associated with the loss of virginity (of one's 'flower') or with the onset of menstruation at puberty, seems to mark the metamorphosis of girls into sexually mature women. As such, it also divides women from men: like anything alien, different, 'other,' it provokes both desire and fear.[5] In 'Combray' there are real flowers, real hawthorns, while the prankquean's 'rosy' and 'paly' ones are only props for a tricky sleight-of-hand, magical, metaphorical signs of purely imaginary possibilities. The metaphorical flowers of *jeunes filles en fleurs* are, among other things, signs of youthful beauty and innocence, while Joyce's menstrual roses are a metaphor that must be taken literally or not at all, signs of a fictional, imaginary anatomy. But Joyce's emphasis on fantasy helps to explain how metaphors work, leading us to take even Proust's elegant, idealizing metaphors 'literally.'

If the prankquean takes the jiminies to the land of the dead, symbolically crucifies them 'with the nail of a top,' baptizes them, and carries them back again under her apron or pinafore (as if she were pregnant), they seem to be reborn through her, as if she were their mother. Who, after all, is their mother? Is the Jarl really their father? The prankquean tale might be trying to explain how children's parents come to be their parents, as if the children were there first. One of its major themes is, in fact, the question of why we need two parents. As Stephen says in *Ulysses,* feigning a child's ignorance of a father's role in producing children: 'Boccaccio's Calandrino was the first and last man who felt himself with child. Fatherhood, in the sense of conscious begetting, is unknown to man... Paternity may be a legal fiction' (U 207). A mother gives birth to, nurses, and takes care of a child, but (Stephen seems to be saying) a father just gets in the way. When the son grows up to be a father, however, he may feel differently, and, fearing the life-and-death powers that mothers seem to possess, he may even try to assert that the 'only begetter' (U 207) of children is a father, not a mother, the Jarl, not the prankquean. The myths of Zeus giving birth to Athena out of his head and to Dionysus out of the 'secret womb' in his thigh try to prove the same thing: Zeus's own father Kronos had a habit of eating up his children, but when Zeus gave him a rock to eat, he threw up all the children he had swallowed, as if giving birth to them once more.

Indeed, the prankquean tale is a battle of the sexes which tries to decide who are more powerful, men or women. And at the same time it tries to figure out what the difference between them really is. The prankquean, asking the Jarl for the pot of porter (please) that he as a good host should give her, also asks him a riddle about the difficulty of telling things apart: 'Why do I am alook alike a poss of porterpease?' She is a lookalike, like the twin jiminies (if they are identical), or like Issy's mirror-self, but is she divided by sexual differences from the Jarl? The pot of porter or peas (pease porridge hot . . .) is also the piss (wit/witter/wittest) that she spills on the Jarl's doorstep before she goes raining in the wilderness. Confusing semen with urine, she wants to know why her piss isn't the same as – and just as good as – his.[6] A man's and a woman's urine look alike, although their urinary organs don't. Throughout *Finnegans Wake,* where the prankquean rains, Anna Livia becomes a river, and Issy tells us to listen to the sound she makes when urinating, a woman's urine becomes a fertile, life-giving, sexually arousing, magically potent substance. The Jarl, who has been busy masturbating (laying warm or cold hands on himself), may simply be drowning in his wet bed; the children in the nursery have an oilcloth sheet to protect their bed, like the oilsheet Stephen's mother puts on his bed on the first page of *A Portrait.* According to the prevailing infantile theory, all sexual activity can be reduced to urinating. When the prankquean pisses on the 'dour' Jarl's doorstep, trying

Marcel, who also has a delicate, sensitive personality, may have borrowed this sensitivity from his mother and grandmother, but Proust – who does not make Marcel a homosexual – adopts, or pretends to adopt, the simplistic, stereotyped view that gentleness, kindness, and sensitivity are feminine:

> Pourquoi, admirant dans le visage de cet homme des délicatesses qui nous touchent, une grâce, un naturel dans l'amabilité comme les hommes n'en ont point, serions-nous désolés d'apprendre que ce jeune homme recherche les boxeurs? Ce sont des aspects différents d'une même réalité (II, 622).

The 'man-woman,' to use Proust's term, is a woman locked inside a man's body, a kind of transsexual who naturally loves the 'opposite' sex, namely men, and whose womanliness, if it is not delicate and graceful, may be shrill, hysterical, and monkey-like.

This theory of congenital androgyny doesn't explain the origins of homosexuality, but it suggests a fundamental paradox: according to Marcel, effeminate homosexuals love manly, virile men who are not homosexuals and cannot love them in return. Marcel assumes that homosexuals, by definition, are not 'manly,' even if, like Charlus with Jupien, they play an aggressive, 'masculine' role, but the example of Charlus, alternately violent and gentle, sadistic and masochistic, reveals a deep-seated uncertainty about 'male' and 'female' roles at the heart of homosexuality. Like Marcel and his tomboyish girlfriends, only more obviously, a homosexual may be narcissistically attracted to idealized, boyish versions of himself, to other men, yet he may unconsciously identify himself with women. Why should a man who doesn't like women be 'effeminate'? The answer, if we can take *Marcel's* childhood as a case in point, seems to lie in the intense ambivalence of a child's early dependence on its mother, the mixture of love and resentment that can grow out of overwhelming need. Uncertain about his own sexual identity, fearing and envying the mysterious, magical powers of the other sex, a boy may wind up playing the part of his mother and looking for others to play the part of himself, loving men only because he loves his mother – and himself – too much.[9] In fact, this scenario could be applied, with the appropriate changes, to any kind of love, since opposites attract but conceal hidden identities, since one tends to love not only oneself but whoever gave – or withheld – the love one through her wit to make him laugh – a traditional fairy-tale motif (see the Grimm brothers' 'The Golden Goose') equates laughter with release from sexual inhibition – he shuts the door in her face, rejecting her advances. But the third time around he opens the door, extends his phallic guns ('to the whole longth of the strength of his bowman's bill'), and violently, thunderously shuts the door again. In short, he shits ('ordurd,' 'shut up shop,' 'shot the shutter'), unless he simply spills more water: 'And they all drank free. . . . And that was the first peace of illiterative porthery in all the flamend floody flatuous world.' Despite the Jarl's noisy, phallic pretensions, the climax of the tale suggests a reversal of sexual roles: the prankquean splashes her fertile urine on the Jarl and he, as if impregnated by her, as if he were Proust's Marcel becoming a mother to his novel, gives birth to a piece of pottery, poetry, or shit. Just as the confusion of semen and urine eliminates the difference between women and men, this infantile 'anal birth' fantasy enables men to give birth as well as women.[7]

Still, the tenuous sexual relations between the Jarl and the prankquean amount to nothing more than a series of ambiguous exchanges. The Jarl ought to offer the prankquean the pot of porter but it is more likely she who offers him the ambiguous drink, the love potion intended for King Mark. He rejects her offer, she steals a jiminy. But in shutting the door, he is also literally handing her an answer – a piece of shit or simply the word *shut*. From one point of view, the Jarl and the prankquean exchange nothing but words. She asks him a riddle or tells a joke in her 'perusienne' dialect and he, answering her in thick Germanic 'dootch,' roaring like thunder, issues a thunderword, a piece of poetry. When Beckett said that *Finnegans Wake* 'is not about something, it is that something itself,'[8] did he mean that it is only about language (how to have fun with words)? Or that words, which seem to signify 'things,' even more than one 'thing' at a time, can take the place of the things they seem to signify? When Joyce has the Jarl 'handword' an answer, he asks us to take that answer literally, as if it were not just a word but a thing. Saying 'shit!' to someone is tantamount to throwing it (hurling abuse, slinging mud), and the idea of 'shitting on' someone is, conversely, a metaphor for expressing contempt. One of the projectors' schemes in *Gulliver's Travels* is to replace words by *things*, having everybody carry a supply of conversational items on his back, but another scheme is to learn propositions by writing them down and eating them, which might have the result of turning words into shit, the 'heaviest,' earthiest, most material thing of all. The prankquean's witty double-entendres may inspire the Jarl to create poetry, but the context suggests that his final, illiterate, 'flatuous' word is just a fart ('git the wind up'), reminding us of Swift's Aeolists (in *A Tale of a Tub*), who are literally inspired by hot air.

As in Swift's case, Joyce's identification of words and things, his anal humor, betrays a serious fear that there is no such thing as 'spirit' after all, that the world is nothing but matter, earth, garbage, rotting corpses, shit. The garbage 'tip' or middenheap or prehistoric barrow where Finn MacCool lies buried, the earth to which dead matter returns, destroys any distinction between the 'waste matter' a man (Earwicker) leaves behind him and the corpse that he finally becomes. As Mulligan says, 'I see them pop off every day in the Mater and Richmond and cut up into tripes in the dissecting room' (U 8). Instead of the pure ether where Icarus would like to soar, there is only 'bad gas': 'they have to bore a hole in the coffins sometimes to let out the bad gas and burn it' (U 104). But this gas is the only spirit or soul a dead man has left: 'Much better to close up all the orifices,' thinks Bloom in the cemetery. 'Yes, also. With wax. The sphincter loose. Seal up all' (U 98). The fear of losing breath or spirit or conscious life stands behind Joyce's lifelong attempt to turn base matter into gold, into air: to give life to the wildest fantasies and turn gross reality into self-sustaining art. Bloom's quasi-scientific interest in physical 'facts,' the impulse behind the 'Ithaca' chapter, is well illustrated by his favorite natural law, the law of falling bodies: everything returns to earth, 'brightness falls from air,' and as Stephen/Icarus decides, 'Not to fall was too hard, too hard' (P 162). ('This was the Fall,' writes Mann in *The Magic Mountain*, 'that first increase in the density of the spiritual, . . .the transition from the insubstantial to the substance.') But everything Joyce wrote is designed to disprove this, to prove that 'Phall if you will, rise you must.' Stephen, who imagines that his 'soul had arisen from the grave of boyhood' (P 170), believes that he can create 'out of the sluggish matter of the earth a new soaring impalpable imperishable being' (P 169) which is, in one sense, himself. Recreating life out of life, Stephen's androgynous artist (in *Ulysses*) not only gives birth to art but, identifying himself with his creation, becomes his own 'consubstantial' son. Godlike, ghostlike, seemingly dead, he may have escaped life's dangers and become invisible, impalpable, immortal, pure spirit.

As Joyce's aloof irony turns to self mocking humor, he describes Shem's writing as his 'wit's waste' and reduces the Jarl's poetry to a piece of shit, as if Keats's ode were identical with the Grecian urn and the urn itself just a piece of 'illiterate pottery.' But his puns do not merely reduce words to material things; they make words seem 'real,' alive, as if in the 'virgin womb' of the imagination the word really could become flesh. Indeed Joyce (in *Finnegans Wake*) specifically identifies words – the spontaneous flow of spoken language – with the babbling sound of the 'river' Anna Livia, with the hissing sound of Issy's micturition, so that the magical, life-giving power of a woman's urine is also the power of language. Just as the prankquean inspires or impregnates the Jarl, Anna Livia pours her babbling flow of words into the ear of sleeping Earwicker – the words of his dream, his 'stream' of consciousness – with the implication that this living, fertile stream (like the whiskey splashed on Finnegan) will wake him up some day. Shem, borrowing his mother's verbal potency, 'lifts the lifewand and the dumb speak' (FW 195), but Joyce's male artists, despite their pretensions of being autonomous, self-sufficient, androgynous creators, seem to need the literal inspiration of a maternal muse. They can create their written (silent) artifacts only by listening to the sound of living voices, particularly women's voices, as if they subscribed to the myth of the written word's dependence on the spoken that Jacques Derrida has been at such pains to dispel.[9] In fact, the Joycean artist, like the Proustian, fears that he himself is dead, alienated from life, that 'life' is something which belongs to others, to the other sex, to mothers, and his whole project is, while insulating himself from life, from other people, to steal that 'life' (Derrida's 'presence') and instill it into his art. So Joyce tries to make *Finnegans Wake* seem as spontaneous, accidental, and alive as possible, as if it were an uncensored stream of consciousness, a babble of voices that has to be heard rather than read, even though it is, in reality, a dense, clotted, carefully constructed verbal artifice that has to be *read* rather than heard. Pretending to imitate the immediacy of life, Joyce either freezes the present moment or lets time flow by in a continuous present, turning the last chapter of *Ulysses* into an unpunctuated stream of consciousness (a woman's). It is Joyce who constructs Molly's monologue, but he pretends to be only recording her words.

If artistic inspiration is sometimes conceived of as a divine afflatus, it may not be too surprising that Joyce's myth of the dreaming father, in *Finnegans Wake,* resembles the medieval legend of 'The Madonna's Conception Through the Ear.'[10] According to the legend, the Virgin Mary was impregnated through the *ear* by the breath or Word of God. In the *Wake* the roles are largely reversed: a woman's words penetrate a man's ear, and it is in the virgin womb of the artist's imagination that the word is made flesh. As we have noted, some medieval paintings show the Virgin Mary being 'impregnated' through the eye, not the ear, by a divine beam of light,[11] and Proust's Marcel, whose eyes are pierced by the light cast from Mme de Guermantes's eyes, who fears the darkness because whatever he can't see may no longer be there, seems to share the belief that light (like the light projected by the magic lantern) is a magical, fertile, almost supernatural substance. Like the Impressionist painters, Proust realizes that we see not the object itself but the (changing) light reflected from it, and yet this does not mean that we are condemned to a world of unstable, unreal appearances: light appears, instead, to be the highly distilled essence of the object, the Joycean *claritas* that the image projects. More mystically, the Berkeleian archdruid in *Finnegans Wake* claims to see the inner light that is *not* reflected from the object, the inner reality or 'inscape,' and in *A Portrait* Stephen decides that he is not interested in the *colors* of words after all. Marcel too implies that the essence of the object is hidden inside it, but ultimately his quasi-platonic essences are the rarefied, refined distillations of a physical, 'sensible' world, tokens of exchange between the world and himself. Like Joyce, Proust would like to turn base matter into light, into air, to make the dense substance of the world almost insubstantial – but not quite, because then it would no longer seem real.[12]

Joyce specifically identifies words with urine as magically fertile substances, but which is a metaphor for which? In the first chapter of *A Portrait,* 'real life' seems to be represented for Stephen by the cold slimy water in the ditch behind the outhouse, the dirty water sucked down a drain, the 'earthy' rainwater of the countryside, and the warm turf-colored bogwater of the bath; these are the signs of the reality that attracts and repels him at the same time. This recurrent, almost obsessive image of 'dirty water,' alternately warm and cold like the bed after he has wet it (P 7), becomes the 'sordid tide of life' (P 98) that threatens to overflow the 'breakwater of order and elegance' that he has erected, that threatens to drown him. Here the 'tide' is merely a metaphor for the squalid disorder of 'real' life, but later he walks near a real breakwater and dreads 'the cold infrahuman odour of the sea' (P 167) as if it might literally drown him: 'O, cripes, I'm drownded!' (P 169) cries one of his friends splashing in the water. In *Ulysses,* where a drowned man is fished from the sea, Stephen's fear of drowning is so great, so irrational, so phobic, that he doesn't even like to wash. It is not simply the sea that he fears but the metaphorical 'tides within him,' the dangerous, uncontrollable impulses that threaten to overwhelm him: 'From without as from within the water had flowed over his barriers' (P 98), just as he couldn't prevent the water from literally wetting his bed. In *Finnegans Wake* the water tends to come from without, from someone else, but it is still identified with bodily fluids.

In short, language seems to take the place of life in *Finnegans Wake,* but words themselves are identified with the sordid, seductive tide of life, as if one could take possession of life (could live) by assimilating words and using them to replace the life they seem to represent. So, in the first chapter of *A Portrait,* Stephen is obsessed not only by squalid images of life but also by the mysterious meanings of words, especially words with more than one meaning, and if words do not always enable him to make sense of reality, they can always be used to construct a new reality (out of the pieces of the old), like the 'green rose' he unwittingly creates out of the wild rose and the green place in the song. Like an alchemist or a primitive shaman, Joyce turns wet, 'dirty,' bodily life into art, but his literal use of metaphor appears to imply that words are literally urine, art is literally shit. Joycean puns (shut/shit, wit/wet) condense more than one meaning, but the point is not that one meaning is 'manifest' and the other 'latent,' one conscious and the other unconscious, one real and the other imaginary. The very idea of metaphor, which makes hypothetical or imaginary possibilities seem real – a sea of dirty water threatening to drown us, a man giving birth to poetry – also translates 'reality' into the signs of fantasy. Joyce's magically fertile substance (urine) signifies, like Proust's precious essences, the animistic 'life' that seems to belong to the world outside oneself, which one has to try to make one's own, and it is the metaphorical possibilities of language – of literature generally – that make this appropriation seem possible.

Jacques Lacan equates metaphor, the substitution of one signifier for another, with the Freudian process of condensation in dreams, in which one signifier is superimposed on another, as in verbal puns.[13]

In this light it might be fruitful to consider metaphor (like the images in dreams)· as a condensation of literal and figurative meanings which undermines the distinction between literal and figurative meaning, a condensation of signifiers in which each one signifies the other. The deliberate confusion of words and 'things' in Joyce's prankquean tale, where verbal 'wit' signifies something wet and the answer 'shut' signifies a piece of shit, is a case in point. For both meanings appear to be 'present,' and it is in fact the interplay between literal and figurative meanings, between *wit* and *wet*, which is the source of the wit, which makes the joke (for the reader) both funny and meaningful.

We have seen how the traditional literary identification of flowers and women (as in the medieval *Roman de la Rose*) becomes in Proust a complex metaphor for sexuality.[14] There are 'real' flowers in the *Recherche,* but the flowers in the phrase *jeunes filles en fleurs* also signify the emerging sexuality of adolescent girls. The metaphor *en fleurs* includes a literal meaning (flowers) and a figurative one (sexuality), but this is not merely an abstract analogy between plants and people. As the corresponding metaphor of 'deflowering' (the same in French) suggests, flowering may signify the presence of a specific, literal 'flower,' the literal sign of an imaginary anatomy. Moreover, the imaginary token of virginity that is lost in the sexual act of 'deflowering' signifies an ephemeral presence that can, by definition, turn into an absence. Reversing the usual rule that males possess visible, prominent sexual organs and females don't, Proust endows women – at least adolescent girls – with an ambiguous sexual possession which men desire to 'steal.' If Marcel finds himself *à l'ombre des jeunes filles en fleurs,* in the *shadow* of these flowers, it may be because – as in the opening pages of the *Recherche* – he is not able to see just what is there and what isn't.

The ephemeral possession signified by the flower becomes finally – like the flower that Joyce's prankquean pulls out of her bag of tricks – the ambiguous sign of the opposite sex, the magical, even illusory 'presence' of the 'other' which one would like to have for oneself. In these terms the male/female dichotomy is reduced to a distinction between self and other, and the self/other dichotomy becomes simply a distinction between presence and absence, the *mana*-filled presence that (because it always belongs to the 'other') is always absent, signified by its own absence. The red/white, rosy/pale contrast in the prankquean tale becomes finally an opposition between colored and 'blank' (Fr. *blanc,* white). These oppositions remind us that the two terms joined in a metaphor are not only similar but different, just as Proust's pink hawthorns are different enough from the white ones to make them seem new and special. By the same token, the present impression (in Proust's metaphorical structure of reminiscence) repeats the past impression, but in a new context, in a new way. The task of the metaphor, according to the Proustian narrator, is to find the 'common essence' uniting the two impressions, to overcome the difference between them (III, 889), but the difference – like the difference between pink and white hawthorns – helps to reveal the essential meaning of the impression, of the hawthorns. The purpose of myth, according to Lévi-Strauss, 'is to provide a logical model capable of overcoming a contradiction,'[15] but we may add that every metaphor is itself a 'logical model' that attempts to overcome a contradiction, the contradiction between two terms that are different yet essentially the same. The opposition between pink and white, rosy and pale, is only a sign of the deeper, more problematical, more uncertain opposition between 'literal' and 'figurative' meanings, between 'real' and 'imaginary' possibilities.[16]

In one sense the metaphor of the flower signifies (condenses) two opposite, reciprocal meanings (presence and absence). We should realize, however, that the 'nothing' that is signified is the elusive, ephemeral 'presence' that metaphor itself tries to bring into being. Derrida justifiably warns us against applying a metaphysics of presence to the universe of the written text, but can we deny that every writer (every text) *tries* to create – out of the difference between signifier and signified, between literal and figurative meanings, between presence and absence – a new presence? A quixotic task? The 'fetishistic' flowers of *jeunes filles en fleurs* – or of the prank-quean – do not really exist, but they are not mere delusions by which Proust or Joyce hides from himself (represses) the painful truth about women.[17] They represent an attempt to understand what women mean to men, to overcome the mysterious 'difference' and disturbing 'otherness' of women. The 'logic' of metaphor makes this possible, not simply by turning 'presence' into a fictional problem rather than a physical one, but by revealing that it – the seductive, elusive, and disturbing presence of the 'other,' of the other sex – always was a fictional problem, a problem of imagination, a problem in the construction and interpretation of signs.

5 Reminiscence, metaphor, and art

The last section of the *Recherche,* occupied with the Princesse de Guermantes's *matinée,* begins in the state of hopeless melancholy which has become habitual for Marcel since early childhood. He returns from a sanatorium uncured, his reading in the Goncourt *Journal* has convinced him of the vanity of literature, and he himself lacks the emotion to respond (as he once did) to the beauty of nature: 'Arbres,... c'est avec froideur, avec ennui que mes yeux constatent la ligne qui sépare votre front lumineux de votre tronc d'ombre' (III, 855), although this is just the kind of subtle boundary between light and shadow that used to mean so much to him. Even his memories of Venice seem like boring, lifeless snapshots (III, 865), mere surface reflections. But at this point, without warning, as he steps out of the way of a car in the courtyard of the Guermantes house, Marcel trips on some uneven pavingstones and feels again the same intense happiness which had been produced in him by the trees near Balbec, the twin steeples of Martinville, the madeleine dipped in tea, and the music of Vinteuil.

The source of this happiness is the recurrence of a physical sensation, the momentary loss of balance which he had also felt, in Venice, as he stood on two uneven stones in the baptistery of St Mark's. A whole miraculous series of finely perceived sense-impressions now assaults Marcel in the Guermantes library, each one evoking some 'resurrection' of the past (as the taste of the madeleine recalled his aunt Léonie's Sunday teas) and enabling him to recover what he thought had been lost. The sound of a spoon knocking against a plate, reminding him of a hammer pounding on a train wheel, brings to his mind the row of trees he had seen from the train. The napkin on which he wipes his mouth, whose stiff, starched quality reminds him of the towel he used at Balbec, recalls for him the view of the sea through his hotel window. And, a few minutes later, the noise of a water pipe, recalling the 'cries' of steamboats approaching Balbec, recreates the memory of a late afternoon in summer in the hotel dining-room, specifically the open windows which make the room itself seem part of the outdoors.

A variety of different sense-impressions initiates the miraculous process of resurrection, including a disturbance in the kinesthetic sense of balance, and each specific memory brings with it a whole train of associations linked to a visual image of the recreated scene. In contrast to the apparently arbitrary, accidental, insignificant quality of the immediate impression, the depth of association is rich, complex, virtually synaesthetic. (In fact, the open front of the hotel dining-room at Balbec, which enables Marcel to step out onto the promenade and join Albertine, which allows indoors and outdoors to merge, exemplifies the dissolution of boundaries which – because it implies the breakdown of the barrier between subject and object – makes aesthetic experience possible.) But the particular reason these moments are so ecstatically joyful is that the apparent abrogation of time – the dissolution of the present in a resurrected past – makes Marcel himself feel (if only in imagination) that he is outside of time, 'un être extra-temporel' (III, 871), and therefore not subject to death (III, 873). Momentarily losing contact with present reality, almost losing consciousness (III, 875), Marcel experiences an ecstatic, synaesthetic sense of fusion – or rather an infusion of rich, sensory life into the depressed, empty self that his dependence on his mother seems to have created 'in' him. But why should the past be more alive, more full of life, more vividly 'present' than the present? Because it exists now only in the imagination, within oneself, under one's control, which is why Marcel's memories of Combray are so happy even when he is remembering how unhappy he was.

In *Beyond the Pleasure Principle* Freud describes a simple game in which a little child throws a reel under a bed and pulls it back again, repeating the words *fort/da* (gone/there), apparently wishing that he could control his mother's comings and goings in the same way.[1] (In a later version of the game, he makes *himself* disappear by hiding from his reflection in a mirror.)[2] In Proust's *Recherche,* Marcel's uncertainty about whether his mother will kiss him goodnight is so disturbing that, after she comes to spend the night with him, he wishes she would go away again. Since her willingness to stay with him is so uncertain, so unpredictable, his ability to manipulate her, his control over her – and over himself – becomes more important than her actual presence. He has tried to convert passive suffering into active control, like the child in the symbolic play-acting of the game, but this reversal of roles is precarious and must be repeated over and over again, in a new, symbolic experience of his own. Freud calls this seemingly irrational need to repeat a painful, even traumatic experience the 'repetition compulsion,' a symptom of a hypothetical self-destructive death instinct, but surely the repetition can be explained by the desire to act out, under one's own authority, an experience that had been threatening and painful.[3] This is one of the motives behind children's play – for example, playing doctor – and it appears to be one of the motives behind art.

In fact, rather than 'acting out' a threatening experience, Marcel tends to recreate it in his mind, in his imagination, where it will no longer be threatening or where he can feel free to savor its dangers in peace. This defensive strategy goes so far that he finds it difficult to enjoy *any* experience unless it has been both lost to present life and remembered in the private kingdom of the imagination:

> Tant de fois, au cours de ma vie, la réalité m'avait déçu parce
> qu'au moment où je la percevais, mon imagination, qui était
> mon seul organe pour jouir de la beauté, ne pouvait s'appliquer à
> elle, en vertu de la loi inévitable que veut qu'on ne puisse
> imaginer que ce qui est absent (III, 872).

The penetration of the past sensation, just as it was, into the present solves this paradox of presence and absence by making the sensation seem real without actually being so (III, 873). Indeed, it is the *pastness* of the past which is so crucial, which for example enables Marcel to recapture the guilt-ridden memory of his dead grandmother, 'car les vrais paradis sont les paradis qu'on a perdus' (III, 870). The unpredictable, uncontrollable quality of real life is threatening to Marcel, as in the episode of his mother's goodnight kiss, but in the case of the reminiscences what is new and unexpected turns out – as he must realize even before he is consciously aware of it – to be old and familiar after all. Reality is assimilated into the imagination, the present into the past, one turning out to be merely a recurrence of the other. As Stephen Dedalus says in Joyce's *Ulysses*, 'He found in the world without as actual what was in his world within as possible' (U 213).

For Marcel, who experiences intense anxiety when he has to stay in strange, unfamiliar hotel-rooms, the task that must be repeated over and over again is to convert whatever is new, alien, different from what he has known, into something familiar and harmless. Not only must he repeat this process forever, like Sisyphus, but the task itself is to make sure that whatever happens merely *repeats* what has gone before. Hence the cyclical structure of Proust's novel, whereby Marcel, claiming to discover the fixed, unvarying laws which govern human existence, becomes the narrator of the novel we have just read, converting the anxieties and disillusionments of real life into the pleasures of art. Marcel is a kind of proto-structuralist who discovers the underlying (synchronic) structure of recurrence in the (diachronic) series of impressions which make up his life, discovering, in fact, that time itself is discontinuous, composed of discrete, separate moments that are finally (in the 'extra-temporal' realm of the imagination) identical.

The joy of making this discovery is initially just the unconscious recognition of something strangely familiar, like the vague and faintly disturbing sense, in *déjà vu,* of having seen something before. As Freud argues in his study of 'the uncanny,' that which seems strange, unfamiliar, and uncanny (Ger. *unheimlich*) may originally have been quite familiar (*heimlich,* 'homely'): the original experience has been repressed, and it is the return of the repressed which seems uncanny.[4] In the case of Marcel's 'reminiscences' at the Hôtel de Guermantes the memory itself seems thoroughly innocent and harmless, but the structure of recurrence is the same: the original experience is not lost, simply forgotten, removed from the field of conscious awareness, and its reemergence is spontaneous, involuntary, beyond conscious control. But the unconscious recognition of familiarity – what else could it be? – is sufficient to make the *unheimlich heimlich* and reassuring after all. Indeed, the physical sensation has no meaning in itself but appears as a sign which, like a hieroglyphic, conceals a hidden truth (III, 878). This hidden truth is not necessarily a dark, repressed, secret 'content,' but simply the structure of recurrence, the inevitable return of unconscious memory, or (more positively) the new-found ability to recreate what one thought one had forgotten. If the present impression is a sign, the memory is also a sign, a half-perceived, half-created reconstruction of the past. In fact, the two signs – two sense-impressions separated from their 'accidental' material causes – are the same sign, the same essential impression, and it is this identification between the two that gives each one its full meaning, evoking the metonymical chain of associations surrounding the original sensation.

And yet the intense joy that Marcel's 'reminiscences' produce in him may seem, to us, a little inflated, a little overstated, as if it were only a temporary, 'manic' illusion of self-possession and immortality – 'toute inquiétude sur l'avenir, tout doute intellectuel étaient dissipés' (III, 866) – no more 'real' than the uncanny sense of anxiety produced by the experience of *déjà vu*. When Marcel finally remembers what it is the madeleine reminds him of – his aunt Léonie's Sunday tea – the discovery, so momentous for him, is perhaps a little disappointing and anticlimactic for us. In other words, Marcel's vivid, sensory-rich reminiscences, which mean more to him than their actual 'content' seems to warrant, seem like 'screen memories,' which conceal as much as they reveal. Serge Doubrovsky has made a good case for the profound wishes and fears that underlie the reminiscence of the madeleine,[5] but the forbidden, disturbing, repressed 'content' surfaces more visibly in the displaced regions of 'Sodom and Gomorrah,' in Marcel's ambivalent life with Albertine, and in the recurrent quasi-primal scenes in which Marcel spies, through literal screens and windows, on homosexual lovers. What is threatening in the reminiscences is simply, as we have said many times before, the dangerously unpredictable quality of everyday life, but Marcel takes the (Freudian) 'psychopathology' of everyday life – here, remembering rather than forgetting – as a proof of unconscious powers, of the existence of a hidden reality beneath its superficial signs. The fusion of reality and imagination, of past and present signs – of signifiers, for the ultimate content signified by these signs remains elusive – exhilarates Marcel because it allows him to overcome the barrier between himself and the outside world that has made him feel lonely, depressed, and only half-alive. He is happy because the world turns out to be inside him but also – and we should be clear about this point – because rich, sensory impressions have penetrated his defenses and the experience has not been so bad after all.

For Marcel, the activity of imagination (and, by the same token, of memory) is not a retreat into private fantasy but an initially passive, then active *assimilation* of reality into terms that he can understand and control. These terms are the pre-existing 'schemas' (to use Piaget's term) of his earlier experiences, experiences that might have seemed threatening when passively suffered but are now part of the symbolic structures that enable him to make sense of the world. To the extent that these earlier experiences remain repressed, merely 'screens' for realizations that are too dangerous, as possibly in the case of the madeleine or of the damp, sooty odor of the little pavilion, to that extent Marcel is condemned to repeat the past, to suffer unsuspected 'returns' of the repressed which he can neither understand nor control. But his willingness to take at least small risks – to surrender to the ecstatic moment and then to analyze it in an effort to pursue its hidden connections with the past, risking the revelations of the latter in order better to understand and thereby control the former – indicates that his model of reminiscence is not merely a regressive return to a fantasized past but an active, 'progressive' search for meanings, even potentially dangerous ones. By the same token, Marcel's minute, painstaking, sometimes painful analysis of his own motives, though it becomes an obsessional defense against letting his feelings run out of control, is also a carefully (rationally) controlled attempt to understand what his feelings really are. He needs to keep life under control, but he is not yet willing to abandon it.

The essence common to the two impressions of the reminiscence – signified by the taste of the madeleine dipped in tea or the cold, damp smell of the little pavilion – is analogous to all the magical, barely material substances that penetrate Marcel's senses in 'aesthetic' experiences: the sound of the musical phrase in Vinteuil's sonata and septet, the color of pink hawthorns, or even light itself, emanating from the eyes of the Duchesse de Guermantes, or from the aptly-named magic lantern, or reflected off the tops of church steeples at sunset. But always the magical substance is the highly distilled essence of the spiritual or material world outside oneself. And yet, once possessed, once 'inside,' this foreign substance always turns out to be, simply, oneself, the mysterious and elusive essence that one likes to think of as one's 'self': as Marcel remarks after tasting the madeleine, 'cette essence n'était pas en moi, elle était moi' (I, 45).

How can we explain this contradiction? As a child Marcel thinks that his mother's presence is a kind of magical essence (signified by her kiss) which he can literally assimilate into himself and without which his life has no real meaning. This magical substance belongs to his mother but (as a kind of 'transitional object' uniting the two of them) can become independent of her, something to comfort him in her absence. And if he manages to possess it, it comes to signify not his mother's presence but his own, a kind of self-presence which convinces him of his own existence. We might say, at the risk of sounding like a parody of contemporary French philosophy, that this presence is the presence of an absence, of an 'other' who is not there or, at the least, will not always be there. Knowing that he cannot fully possess his mother, that he cannot even keep her in his room, Marcel 'valorizes' these 'transitional,' volatile essences, endows them with magical significance, and attempts to incorporate them into himself in the hope of achieving that sense of plenitude, presence, and (even) identity that only his *mother's* original presence would seem to be able to provide. If this infantile strategy seems like some deterministic oral 'fixation,' it would be more accurate to say that Marcel's early separation anxiety creates the conditions (the 'schemas' or structures) for his later aesthetic and sensory experiences.

The penetration of this magical, life-giving essence through various sensory channels does not merely nourish Marcel, keep him alive, as if it were the oral assimilation of his mother's milk, tea, or 'presence,' but (like the Madonna's 'conception through the eye') inspires, fertilizes, impregnates him, creating a kind of magical, 'hysterical' pregnancy, conferring upon him the magical powers of a mother, enabling him (after a long period of gestation) to give birth to art. In a certain sense, the life-giving *mana* turns out to be a dangerous foreign substance after all, a poison which has to be expelled, in the form of the child that is born, the work of art, but only at the cost of the artist-mother's life. As the example of his grandmother makes clear, the life of another person, even the intensely 'alive' memory of his grandmother, cannot become part of the self until it is apparently lost forever, dead, as if life were a virulent organism that had to be killed off before it could be assimilated. The reminiscence-like 'intermittences' of the heart – the temporal structure of 'mourning and melancholia' – remind us that the problem is not only the loss of the other person but the guilt this loss may create or recreate in us. Marcel plays the part of a cannibal who kills his enemies in order to 'eat' them, eats them in order to possess their spirits, except that his 'enemies' are those he loves best. Even this 'dead,' assimilated virus of otherness is so dangerous that it has to be expelled again, but, deprived of 'life,' the patient dies.

According to this magical, pseudo-scientific conception, life is dangerous in large quantities, it must be taken in small, homeopathic doses, and only the 'killed' vaccine is safe. It is on such magical theories that 'neurasthenia,' hypochondria, or for that matter neurosis is based, but Marcel proves his case by succumbing to an imaginary disease.

Moreover, Marcel, Proust's spokesman on art, identifies the magical, life-giving 'essence' that inspires or impregnates him – the essence common to the two impressions of the reminiscence – with the concept of metaphor, as if the translation of 'essence' into language were the initial (and essential) symbol-making activity of art. In his description of the Martinville steeples, the narrator, citing his own youthful account of the episode – transposed from Proust's pre-*Recherche* description of the twin steeples of Caen – diffidently suggests that 'ce qui était caché derrière les clochers de Martinville devait être quelque chose d'analogue à une jolie phrase' (I, 181). And yet Marcel, moved by the mellifluous, lulling sound of his mother's reading of *François le Champi*, pays hardly any attention to the words. Like Swann, he admires Vinteuil's music because it *is* so ineffable, so spiritual, so sublime – immaterial and untranslatable – suggesting a direct 'communicaton des âmes' (III, 258) quite unlike language. In fact, Marcel specifically condemns the kind of superficial realism, represented by the passage from the Goncourt journal, that claims to mirror 'life' and identifies this kind of surface literalism with photography and film, as if movies could not be as mysterious and beautiful as magic lanterns and as if cinematography could not develop techniques like flashbacks, dissolves, intercutting, and montage: 'Quelques-uns voulaient que le roman fût une sorte de défilé cinématographique des choses. Cette conception était absurde. Rien ne s'éloigne plus de ce que nous avons perçu en réalité qu'une telle vue cinématographique' (III, 882-3). Marcel admires Bergotte's writing not only for what it says but for its musical, flowing, old-fashioned style (I, 93-4), although M. de Norpois disparages Bergotte as a 'flute-player' and Marcel himself gradually loses interest in him. Yet, just before he dies, Bergotte goes to see Vermeer's *View of Delft* at an exhibition of Dutch paintings and is deeply moved by the simple, self-sufficient beauty of a little patch of yellow wall. He himself may never have written anything so beautiful, but still he feels that he has 'imprudently' given his life for the little patch of wall, for beauty, for art (III, 187). Despite its visible, realistic, representational quality, in its epiphany-like clarity and self-sufficiency the *petit pan de mur jaune* reminds us of the musical *petite phrase* of Vinteuil, whose septet, in turn, is tinged with a quasi-material, painterly redness. Yet the fact that Proust himself loved Vermeer's painting, went to just such an exhibition at the Jeu de Paume, experienced an attack like Bergotte's, and wrote this passage on Bergotte's death immediately after suggests that he may have shared Bergotte's anxiety about exchanging life for art.[6]

Certainly Proust's spokesman, Marcel, exalts the imagination and speaks with an almost Swiftian misanthropy of the worthlessness of love, friendship, and social relations. And the kind of art represented by Bergotte's stylized writing, Vinteuil's 'transcendental' music, and Elstir's Impressionistic paintings, in which the land and the sea seem to merge, seems to be less concerned with material, representational 'content' than with the pure, harmonious form that melts distinctions and boundaries, just as the magic lantern transforms all material objects into the same visual images: Elstir, 'comparant la terre à la mer, supprimait entre elles toute démarcation . . . le peintre avait su habituer les yeux à ne pas reconnaître de frontière fixe, de démarcation absolue, entre la terre et l'océan' (I, 836). As we have noted many times, this Impressionistic dissolution of boundaries – represented, analogously, by the smooth, flowing, unbroken sound of his mother's voice reading from *François le Champi,* the old tombstones in the Combray church overflowing their borders like honey, and the three steeples of Martinville and Vieuxvicq merging and dissolving into the night – pleases Marcel because of his own particular anxieties about separation and fusion, suggesting that the apparently impenetrable barrier between himself and the outside world might simply melt away, that his mother's soft, lulling presence might simply enter his ears through her voice. By the same token, Proust praises Flaubert's continuous, monotonous, hermetic, even dull style (in an article published in 1920) for being so pure and homogeneous, for being a kind of conveyor belt ('Trottoir roulant' or moving sidewalk) which sweeps the reader along its inexorable path.[7]

But if there is no line of demarcation, in Elstir's paintings, between the land and the sea, there still is one (in Marcel's mind) between the church and the rest of Combray (I, 62-3). For Marcel *needs* barriers, boundaries, and lines of separation to prevent the outside world from rushing in and overwhelming him, whereby everything (including his own inner 'self') might be swallowed up and lost in a total, formless fusion. While reading in the garden at Combray, engrossed in a book, he feels that even his mind, his self-consciousness, forms a thin layer between him and any external object, just as Virginia Woolf claims that life surrounds *us* like 'a luminous halo, a semi-transparent envelope': 'Quand je voyais un objet extérieur, la conscience que je le voyais restait entre moi et lui, le bordait d'un mince liséré spirituel qui m'empêchait de jamais toucher directement sa matière...' (I, 84). Marcel would like to cross through this thin border, to see objects as they 'really' are, as if actually touching them, but he rejects 'naive realism' and (I think) takes comfort in the fact that his 'mind' can insulate him from objects. There is even a 'thin partition' (or at least a transparent window) between him and potential 'primal scenes,' between him and his grandmother at Balbec. In short, separation appeals to Marcel as much as fusion, because each alternative reflects one aspect of his own ambivalent feelings: as in the example of the 'carafes' in the Vivonne, 'remplies par la rivière où elles sont à leur tour encloses, à la fois "contenant" aux flancs transparents comme une eau durcie et "contenu" plongé dans un plus grand contenant de cristal liquide et courant' (I, 168), where the glass border is a kind of ambiguous Moebius-strip surface dividing inner and outer spaces of water, and where the water and glass resemble each other, making the line of demarcation between *them* that much more uncertain. Likewise, the famous 'deux côtés' of Guermantes and Méséglise seem permanently, eternally separate, as if shut up 'dans les vases clos et sans communication entre eux d'après-midi differents' (I, 135), but each path does circle back on the other and, figuratively, the two paths of Swann and the Guermantes come to intersect each other many times.

Elstir's paintings themselves – the most numerous and extended examples of art in Proust's novel – do not merely dissolve boundaries and bathe the world in a luminous glow. On the contrary, they virtually 'recreate' the world by extracting, 'du chaos que sont toutes choses que nous voyons,' isolated images detached and set apart from everything else (I, 834), like Vermeer's little patch of yellow wall or like the discrete, self-contained images that become Stephen Dedalus's epiphanies. In Joyce's *Portrait of the Artist as a Young Man*, Stephen Dedalus makes it clear that the artist embraces life only at a discreet distance. The separation of subject and object, which might imply the radical isolation and alienation of the self, a rationalization for Stephen's withdrawal into himself, becomes an aesthetic principle whereby the artist is mysteriously united with the beautiful object. The aesthetic image remains for Stephen a 'thing,' a discrete object, whose hard-edged, clear-cut boundaries prevent the image from merging into its background: 'The first phase of apprehension is a bounding line drawn about the object to be apprehended,' which appears as 'selfbounded and selfcontained upon the immeasurable background of space or time which is not it' (P 212). This clear-focus, high-definition technique, masquerading as photo-realism – 'the gropings of a spiritual eye which seeks to adjust its vision to an exact focus' (SH 211) – seems quite different from Woolf's luminous haloes, and yet it too produces a kind of luminous glow in the observer, 'the luminous silent stasis of esthetic pleasure' (P 213). In other words, for all its down-to-earth *whatness,* the radiant *claritas* of the image belongs as much to the imagination which perceives it as to the thing itself. Stephen's detached, impersonal artist – 'invisible, refined out of existence,' like the God of creation – clings to the clear reality of the image, but it *is* an image that Stephen exalts, the epiphany-like impression of the object on a human subject. Stephen may not live up to his Flaubertian ideal of the lofty, impersonal, invisible artist – when he writes a poem in homage to a 'temptress,' he feels as if 'his soul had passed from ecstasy to languor' (P 223) – but his professed principle of aesthetic detachment is, like Eliot's doctrine of the impersonal poet translating emotion into 'objective correlatives,' typical of modernist aesthetics. Of course this modernism begins at least with Flaubert, and it is not hard to find Pateresque, even Shelleyan imagery and 'dissolving moments of virginal selfsurrender' (P 152) in Joyce's twentieth-century *Portrait of the Artist.* Still, Stephen's dissolving moments are hedged with sympathetic irony, and in describing them Joyce might be playing the role of the impersonal, invisible artist painting the portrait of the artist *as a young man.* (Joyce plays it both ways.)

In a similar way, the Impressionism of Proust's character Elstir appears to be not merely a blurring of vision but a precise, carefully controlled technique. Elstir's images undergo a kind of metamorphosis – 'analogue à celle qu'en poésie on nomme métaphore' (I, 835), says Marcel – whereby they are transformed from our conventional representation of them into our original, immediate, sensory impression of them: 'selon ces illusions optiques dont notre vision première est faite' (I, 838). It is this kind of metamorphosis, not merely a dissolution of boundaries, that makes Elstir, in his picture of Carquethuit harbor, paint the town in 'marine terms' and the sea in 'urban terms,' just as a poet might describe church steeples in terms of the masts of ships or young girls in terms of blossoming flowers. The intermingling of the land and the sea seems (in linguistic terms) like a metonymical displacement from one to the other, but the exchange of signs between two completely different things, the transformation of one into the other, is (according to Marcel) a process of metaphorical substitution. Even the isolated images that Elstir seems to extract from the world around him are not just random snapshots but, in effect, metaphors for real things, representations of what they are 'really' like beneath the deceptive appearances of the 'naive realism' that we have grown accustomed to: 'si Dieu le Père avait créé les choses en les nommant, c'est en leur ôtant leur nom, ou en leur en donnant un autre, qu'Elstir les recréait' (I, 835). The 'optical illusions' which the artist (re-) discovers and (re-)creates are not adolescent idealizations that turn out to be false illusions like the ones Marcel is forced to outgrow. On the contrary, they reflect a freshness and innocence of vision which undermines metaphysical assumptions about 'objectivity' and restores, instead, a childlike, 'phenomenalist' perception of the world. Is this reality? Is this truth? Or is it simply the artist's private, subjective vision? In a slightly different sense, Marcel ascribes this representation of immediate, subjective, emotional experience, in all its apparent contradiction and confusion – like his 'running commentary' description of the Martinville steeples (with which he almost collides) from a constantly changing point of view – to Dostoyevsky. So, too, Elstir's portrait of 'Miss Sacripant,' rather than merely blurring the distinction between male and female, endows one with the 'signs' and attributes of the other, transforms one into the other, and turns that boyish, girlish face topped with short hair into a metaphor for (the idea of) the opposite sex, for the ambiguity of sexual identity. In short, Elstir's paintings are not strictly realistic but neither do they abandon reality for a strictly imaginary world; instead, they transform ambiguous images into signs or metaphors of a hidden, underlying reality.

As Proust finally formulates it, the task of the artist is not simply to escape into a world of private fantasy, no matter how beautiful – which Marcel's figurative, highly subjective description of Vinteuil's music might suggest – but to discover the hidden reality beneath or behind or within the tantalizing though deceptive signs of everyday experience. In a passage whose last line we have quoted before, Marcel says:

> déjà à Combray je fixais avec attention devant mon esprit quelque image qui m'avait forcé à la regarder, un image, un triangle, un clocher, une fleur, un caillou, en sentant qu'il y avait peut-être sous ces signes quelque chose de tout autre que je devais tâcher de découvrir, une pensée qu'ils traduisaient à la façon de ces caractères hiéroglyphiques qu'on croirait représenter seulement des objets matériels. Sans doute ce déchiffrage était difficile, mais seul il donnait quelque vérité a lire (III, 878).

The reading, the decipherment of these hieroglyphic-like signs is the first step in the process of writing. The writer must first 'read' the signs around him, translating the secret hidden in the Martinville steeples into the 'jolie phrase' which is somehow analogous to it. In the case of the epiphany-like reminiscences, charged with hidden, unconscious significance, the writer must first rediscover the *original* impression and then link the two in an appropriate 'phrase': 'Ce que nous appelons la réalité est un certain rapport entre ces sensations et ces souvenirs qui nous entourent simultanément . . . rapport unique que l'écrivain doit retrouver pour en enchaîner à jamais dans sa phrase les deux termes différents' (III, 889). (On the one hand, our memories seem to surround us like a hazy cloud – another case of vague, diffuse boundaries – but, by the same token, the two 'terms' of a reminiscence are radically separated in time.) The writer's prototypical phrase, a microcosm of the writer's own style, analogous to the musical *petite phrase* of Vinteuil or even Vermeer's *petit pan de mur jaune,* is, in effect, a metaphor for the hidden meaning of the reminiscence: 'en rapprochant une qualité commune à deux sensations, il dégagera leur essence commune en les réunissant l'une et l'autre pour les soustraire aux contingences du temps, dans une métaphore' (III, 889).

But how is this common quality, this common essence, translated into a metaphor? Is it sufficient, as the narrator says, to take two different objects, establish their relation, and 'les enfermera dans les anneaux nécessaires d'un beau style,' *enclosing* everything in decorative, ornamental, or at least homogeneous language? As in the case of the memories that 'surround' us, a paradigmatic, signifying relation is being confused with mere spatial or syntagmatic contiguity, so that Marcel's examples of metaphor at the end of this paragraph – recognizing 'la beauté d'une chose [only] dans une autre,' noon at Combray in the sound of churchbells, mornings at Doncières in the sound of the heater – are simply 'metonymical' associations. But, as in Elstir's paintings, the line between metaphor and metonymy, to borrow Proust's own metaphor for 'metonymical' contiguity, is not always clear. Because of his (ambivalent) fondness for boundaries, Marcel likes the idea of enclosing *things* in unbroken rings of *words,* of sealing them off within his own personal (linguistic) style. And yet he recognizes that the writer's words, rather than merely surrounding objects, can represent or signify the (metaphorical) relations between them. The 'rapport' between current sensations and memories, between two sensations separated in time, is not the only possible example of two different 'things' possessing a common quality, but the Proustian narrator uses this prototypical example of the reminiscences as, in effect, a metaphor for metaphor. And, implicitly, he uses 'metaphor' to mean not just the sign of a common property, of an identification between two 'things,' but the verbal sign of the reality hidden behind or within the phenomenal 'sign' of the natural object, revealing its true significance or 'identity.' Thus the reminiscences are a metaphor for metaphor, and 'metaphor' is a metaphor for signification, for the essential artistic process of 'reading' (deciphering) the phenomenal sign and 'translating' it into a verbal one: 'Le devoir et la tâche d'un écrivain sont ceux d'un traducteur' (III, 890). And if reading, decipherment, and translation are metaphors for the process of artistic creation, the implication is that creation is not 'invention' – sheer fantasy – but a deliberate, step-by-step process of interpretation and representation, whereby one seeks to interpret the true significance of phenomenal signs in order to represent them by means of verbal signs.[8]

The relation between criticism and creation, between reading and writing, is familiar from Proust's earlier work – including *Contre Sainte-Beuve,* Proust's pastiches of other writers, his translations of Ruskin, and even his early essay on reading, *Journées de lecture.* And the conclusion we must draw is not only that criticism, even reading itself, may be creative, but that artistic creation (writing) includes, depends upon, and requires, reading, interpretation, and 'translation.' 'L'impression est pour l'écrivain ce qu'est l'expérimentation pour le savant,' says Marcel, suggesting that the act of interpreting the impression is an analytical, rational, even scientific activity, 'avec cette différence que chez le savant le travail de l'intelligence précède et chez l'écrivain vient après' (III, 880).[9] A few pages further on, Marcel claims that the metaphorical relation between objects or impressions is 'analogue dans le monde de l'art à celui qu'est le rapport unique de la loi causale dans le monde de la science' (III, 889). In the world of art, there are no objective, physical laws, only symbolic relations – unless the artist attempts to imitate the workings of the phenomenal world. Instead of a strictly deterministic causal relationship between past and present events, the artist affirms simply a resemblance, a common property, a sense of *déjà vu*. Or rather, in Marcel's case, he *discovers* this resemblance in the spontaneous recurrence of an earlier impression, discovering not a physical law but a psychological one, whether we call it the 'return of the repressed' (Freud) or ascribe it, more generally, to the genetic, structural principle that we perceive the world in terms of our own past experience. Indeed, the sudden, intense, even dizzying emotional surrender to an 'impression,' which affects Marcel so deeply, is not sufficient to turn him into an artist. After the reminiscence of the madeleine, after the episode of the Martinville steeples, Marcel feels that he has not yet fully penetrated the secret of the impression, solved the mystery, discovered why he is so happy – despite the fact that he has located the source of the reminiscence and attempted to translate the 'impression' into words. The arduous, burdensome task of analyzing, interpreting, understanding the impression – the quasi-scientific work of the 'intelligence' – is begun but never completed, always postponed to some indefinite future, and for this reason Marcel cannot believe that he will ever be a writer. Instead, finding himself waxing ecstatic over musty odors – foolishly, irrationally, inexplicably – he feels that he is wasting his life.

Only after the final reminiscences at the Hôtel de Guermantes does he explicitly formulate his explanation of the relations between art and life, his theory that the 'essence' of an impression – the meaning it has for him, for a human subject – can be liberated from time and represented in language. Besides, explaining how a work of art is created is not the same as actually creating one. After his discovery, after his decision to renounce the world and devote his life to art, Marcel still has to go back to his room and write the book that is germinating inside him: line by line, sentence by sentence, 'weaving' the impressions, the reminiscences, the 'screen memories' and 'primal scenes' – which figure most prominently in the first and last volumes – into a more extended discursive structure of analysis, explanation, and commentary. After all, Proust himself had already written numerous manuscript versions of the reminiscences before writing – before being able to write – *A la Recherche du temps perdu*. The problem, as many critics have pointed out, was to integrate the metaphorical-symbolic reminiscences into a more discursive metonymical-syntagmatic narrative. But perhaps the discovery of this metaphorical-symbolic relation (between random, accidental 'impressions'), the realization that his personal, subjective, idiosyn-cratic experiences obey universal psychological 'laws,' was exactly what enabled him – what 'will' enable his surrogate Marcel – to write his book. For the personal, 'subjective' vision of the artist – who renounces absolute objectivity and admits that 'Elle était bien gentille' means only 'J'avais du plaisir à l'embrasser' (III, 896) – is itself a guarantee of 'truth,' of the 'différence qualitative qu'il y a dans la façon dont nous apparaît le monde, différence qui, s'il n'y avait pas l'art, resterait le secret éternel de chacun' (III, 895). It is his confidence in psychological laws, in the validity of personal experience, that enables him to write about society, about men and women, about heterosexuals and homosexuals, and – with the novelist's freedom to reconstruct and recreate – about himself. The artist's vision reflects his own way of seeing things, the symbolic structures through which ;he both perceives the world and creates his art, but it is precisely through such personal, individual constructions that we can discover the underlying principles that 'govern' the relations between one person and another, between fantasy and reality, between selves and worlds. Even if the reader is a homosexual and the writer a heterosexual, or *vice versa*:

> En réalité, chaque lecteur est, quand il lit, le propre lecteur de soi-même. L'ouvrage de l'écrivain n'est qu'une espèce d'instru-ment optique qu'il offre au lecteur afin de lui permettre de discerner ce que, sans ce livre, il n'eût peut-être pas vu en soi-même (III, 911).

In a sense each work of art, too, is an experiment: for the writer,

an experiment in constructing symbolic structures that will represent the world as he perceives it, his relation with the world, or
simply his fantasies about the world and about himself; for the
reader-critic, an experiment in analyzing, interpreting, and explaining this symbolic construction. But a writer who treats the world as
a text that has to be deciphered has already begun the critic's work
of reading, decipherment, interpretation, and 'deconstruction,'
except that the signs are no longer 'natural' but verbal and the
symbols (the metaphorical-symbolic relations that he both discovers
and creates) are not *ours* but *his*. From this point of view there is not
much difference between criticism and 'art' except that criticism
carries through the process of interpretation that art only sometimes
begins: 'deconstruction' has priority over 'construction,' and the
'best,' most modern, most *written* texts are those self-deconstructing
verbal 'structures' that reveal their own textual properties, their own
'signifying' status in the endless interplay of signs.[10] There is much
'truth' in this argument, and this point of view undermines many
romantic-idealistic illusions about artistic creation and imagination.
However, despite Marcel's repeated emphasis upon the decipherment and translation of signs, Proust's *Recherche* is not simply a
self-reflexive, post-modern word-game, constructing and decon-
structing itself forever, at random, without the apparent intervention of an author. Indeed, following his own prescriptions in the
article on Flaubert's style, Proust's own rich, complex, languorous
style – a perfectly controlled, homogeneous and almost endless
stream of words – seems to dissolve imperfections, melt down
impurities, and translate everything into its own unique 'substance,'
its own verbal 'essence': as if the task of the artist were simply to
dissolve boundaries, provide a sense of harmonious merger, and let
all things flow (slowly), rather than to break up his own text, to
reveal its gaps and fissures, to 'deconstruct' it.

But this is a caricature: Proust's style seems like a beautiful,
meaningless, non-signifying stream of words only if we read it – like
Marcel listening to his mother's reading of *François le Champi* – without paying attention to the words. Even in the article on Flaubert,
Proust says, without conceding a single 'beautiful' metaphor to
Flaubert himself: 'je crois que la métaphore seule peut donner une
sorte d'éternité au style.'[11] And in the *Recherche,* referring to the
metaphorical relation between two 'impressions,' Marcel declares:
'Le rapport peut être peu intéressant, les objets médiocres, le style

mauvais, mais tant qu'il n'y a pas en cela, il n'y a rien' (III, 890). The opposition between criticism and creation, between reading and writing, between the work of 'intelligence' and the work of 'imagination' – which becomes, in the text itself, an (ambiguous and uncertain) distinction between the metonymical-discursive context of the narrative and the metaphorical-symbolic structure of reminiscence – reflects finally Marcel's reciprocal desires to assimilate the outside world (into himself) and to construct a new world out of (inside) himself. Analyzing, interpreting, deciphering the 'metaphorical' relations that he discovers in the 'signs' around him, he nonetheless invents – out of the structures of personal experience – a 'new' metaphorical relation between himself and his art, a virtual myth of artistic creation in which the artist-mother dies so that his 'child,' his novel, may be born. And yet, despite this apparent 'sublimation' of life into art, the Proustian myth of artistic creation signifies neither an absolute idealization of art nor a total renunciation of life.

6 Proust's myth of artistic creation

The irrational, inexplicable pleasure that comes to Marcel in certain privileged moments, the almost manic ecstasy of the reminiscences in which a chronic sense of depression (compounded of loneliness, purposelessness, and the deathlike inertia of *l'habitude*) gives way to a sudden feeling of self-worth, self-sufficiency, and immortality, acts, according to Marcel, 'de la même façon qu'opère l'amour, en me remplissant d'une essence précieuse' (I, 45). This essence seems to invade him, to penetrate his senses from the outside, but it is no longer – if it ever was – in the external object. Now it is in himself, 'ou plutôt cette essence n'était pas en moi, elle était moi' (I, 45). The essence that seems to come to him from the outside also seems to rise up from somewhere deep within him, from some dark internal region inaccessible to consciousness, and this return of an unconscious memory allows him to recover and repossess his own past self, making him feel that there *is* a permanent identity which overrides temporal discontinuities. But if this pleasure reminds him of love, of the feeling of being in love, it might be because the 'essence' of the beloved person has seemed to enter into him, to merge with him, to become the essence of himself that he calls 'moi.' So the 'essence' of a special impression seems to be a kind of 'transitional phenomenon' – to use again the terminology of the British child-psychologist D. W. Winnicott – located in the ambiguous inner/outer space of a 'symbiotic' mother-child relationship, just as Marcel's mother's kiss comes to signify her presence when she's not around, a volatile presence that he can take possession of and assimilate into himself. The attempt to 'possess' his mother is active and deliberate, while the sudden infusion of the essence is felt (passively) as a penetration from the outside, but in either case the blurring of boundaries suggests a fusion between inner and outer worlds. Marcel assimilates the essence into himself, identifies it with 'himself,' attempts to discover its origin and to explain its miraculous effect on him, in an effort to take control of it, render it less threatening, restore his sense of boundaries, and resume control over *himself.* But the fact remains that it is the sudden, unexpected sense of fusion – between subject and object, between inner and outer worlds, between himself and his mother – that gives him such an irrational, inexplicable feeling of pleasure.

In short, Marcel's special moments are somewhat domesticated versions of the experience the Romantics called sublime:[1] instead of surrendering to or identifying with an all-encompassing power or presence (usually Nature), Marcel assimilates a specific phenomenal (natural) essence – taste or sound or odor – that seems to be the sign of some hidden presence, some deeper meaning. And the possession of this essence endows him with the mysterious creative power of the artist (the Romantic Imagination). Marcel's emphasis upon the self's creative powers – 'Chercher? pas seulement: créer' (I, 45) – belongs to the 'egotistical' (Wordsworthian) mode of the sublime, but the specific essence – the damp, moldy odor of the pavilion or even the 'perfume' of the madeleine dipped in tea – is humble, trivial, down-to-earth, hardly 'sublime' in appearance. After Flaubert's attempt to find beauty in the most trivial or ugly details, after almost a century of French realism, Proust's post-Romantic emphasis upon the 'impression,' the apparently insignificant specificity of the event, is much closer to the modernist version of the sublime represented by the Joycean epiphany. The impression is only a sign of something hidden 'within' the object, but by the same token the impression *is* significant: it reveals as well as conceals its secret meaning. Proust's essences are not simply transcendental, Platonic ideas imprisoned in, and distorted by, material objects, despite the attraction this Platonic model has for Proust. They are much more like the magical, animistic *mana* – a childlike concept as well as a 'primitive' one – that seems to reside in objects and yet can cross over the material boundary of objects, less abstract and more 'concrete' than the rationalistic Platonic concept.[2] Proust's 'concrete' specificity ensures that the 'sublime' pleasure of the impression does *not* simply fulfill a regressive, narcissistic fantasy of merging with one's mother. Though the sublime moment (for Proust) is 'extratemporal,' allowing Marcel to 'escape' from time, the apparent fusion is momentary, transient, unstable: boundaries become permeable, insides and outsides get confused, but then the self reasserts its autonomy and control.

Indeed, despite the apparently harmless triviality of the impression, its sudden, unexpected, inexplicable, *involuntary* character makes it seem like (feel like) a surrender to powerful (invading) forces beyond one's control, as in the inexplicable, exaggerated, irrational, 'uncanny' fear or terror that represents the 'negative' pole of the sublime. It is the equilibrium between this anxiety-provoking sense of change and the reassuring discovery of repetition, between the surrender to external danger and the assimilation of magical power, that makes the reminiscences so pleasurable, so exhilarating, so 'sublime.' And yet Marcel does not simply overcome the danger: on the contrary, he succumbs to the threat of change, accepts the imminence of death, and thereby escapes the anxiety of not knowing what will happen. Like his aunt Léonie, he chooses death so that it will not choose him, except that Léonie is only pretending to be dead, trying to cheat death, and Marcel (at least in this sense) isn't. His death, his withdrawal from life, is a necessary precondition for his conversion into an artist.

I

When Morel gives a concert at the Verdurins', Charlus displaces the mistress, adopts the role of the hostess, and invites his own (aristocratic) guests, who have no manners and snobbishly snub Mme Verdurin, but she pays him back (in a repetition of Swann's affair with Odette) by banishing the noble Charlus and taking to her bosom the plebeian artist Morel. Charlus falls deeper and deeper into his secret underworld, getting arrested because of his association with the wartime deserter Morel and winding up an infantile caricature of himself, cared for by his nurse Jupien, who has to prevent him from accosting young boys. But this is only one example of Proust's law of social change, which follows not justice but the eternal cycle of the wheel of fortune. Charlus falls, the Duchesse de Guermantes (opening her house to writers and actresses) becomes *déclassée,* while such social upstarts as Bloch, Rachel, and Morel become successful artists, not necessarily because they have talent. Odette becomes the mistress of the Duc de Guermantes, and, according to the uncorrected text of *La Fugitive,* Gilberte, who has already married Saint-Loup, is destined to become the next Duchesse de Guermantes. Mme Verdurin, after two more marriages, becomes the latest Princesse de Guermantes and, minus her original husband, reigns supreme over the social world. We can imagine her as an old, weird sister, one of the Fates, devouring her enemies as well as her husbands, presiding over the rises and falls of social change as if she herself would never die. Her secret, like Odette's, is simply that she has survived, outlasting her rivals, magically killing them off like a wicked stepmother in a fairy-tale.

Proust's law of change provides us with a series of dramatic reversals and discoveries (analogous to the miraculous reminiscences) in which characters shed their false appearances – the superficial roles they play in society – and show us what they 'really' are. The old music-teacher, Vinteuil, turns out to be the great composer of the same name, the foolish M. Biche of the Verdurin set turns out to be the great painter Elstir, and even the rich, empty-headed sportsman, Octave, Andrée's future husband, turns out to be a true artist, a brilliant costume- and set-designer. The Dreyfus case creates predictable social divisions, but, in another surprising reversal, the Prince de Guermantes, a reactionary anti-Semite who makes an exception of his friend Swann, becomes convinced, despite his own private prejudices, that Dreyfus is innocent. Not so surprisingly, the 'liberal' aristocrat Saint-Loup, who borrows his pro-Dreyfus sentiments from his mistress Rachel, gives them up when he gives her up. All things change, according to Proust, but the more they change the more they remain the same, revealing their true natures, their secret 'essences.' The wheel of fortune implies not only change but repetition, each person playing his part in a predictable pattern of events which should not surprise us as much as it does. In the closing party at the Princesse de Guermantes's, everyone has grown old or died, the Faubourg Saint-Germain is filled with *parvenus,* the Duchess thinks of Marcel as one of her oldest friends, the Princess herself is an 'impostor,' but this is how it always was, the slow process of change and assimilation speeded up by the war and by Proust's Balzacian taste for exaggeration, caricature, and melodrama. The first Guermantes was also presumably a *parvenu,* an impostor, but social memory is not that long and everyone has forgotten.

The cycle of social change, which prescribes that each prince or princess must give way to another, implies that each individual must die for the sake of social continuity. The customers in Jupien's brothel, the citizens of Paris who descend into the catacomb-like tunnels of the Metro to take their pleasure while the bombs are falling outside, are like the citizens of Pompeii or Sodom, but Proust's vain, frivolous, self-seeking 'socialites' are always oblivious to death, refusing to take notice of anyone else's – except to congratulate themselves for having survived – in order to ignore the possibility of their own. In the famous incident of the red shoes, the Duc de Guermantes, in order to avoid being late to a dinner-party, cuts short Swann's discussion of his own impending death but, discovering that his wife's shoes do not match her dress, decides that she has time to change them. The Duke's cousin 'Mama' is on his deathbed, but the Duke, unwilling to let a death in the family prevent him from attending a costume ball later that night, though warned by two old sisters armed with walking-sticks (the Fates again), finally pretends that the news of his cousin's death is 'exaggerated.' M. Verdurin, in order not to cancel his own dinner-party, says exactly the same thing when told of the death of Princess Sherbatoff, the most faithful of the faithful, and Mme Verdurin pretends that she never really liked her. (In one more surprising reversal, which demonstrates that appearances are deceptive and truth contradictory, after Saniette, their personal scapegoat, the butt of a thousand cruel jokes, loses all his money and has a stroke, the Verdurins decide to support him secretly for the few years he has left to live, pretending that the money has been left to him by none other than Princess Sherbatoff.) In another variation of the red shoes motif, Prof. E—, who is neurotically compulsive about running his own elevator, barely agrees to give Marcel's dying grandmother a hasty examination because he is dining out, he is in a hurry, and his buttonhole needs to be fixed. The moral of this black comedy, this dance of death where the living blithely dance on the graves of their 'friends' and relatives, is that social ties do not really bind people together, that we die as we live, alone.

The disguises which the Prince and the guests at the Guermantes party seem to wear, which make them seem like actors or even puppets, suggest that the effect of time, of growing older, is not gradual and imperceptible but an insect-like metamorphosis from one form into another. These doddering old creatures are caricatures of their former selves, and the lesson of their transformations is that their former selves are dead, that their current, white-haired selves will also die. The implication, in the 'reminiscences,' that past and present images are identical is cause for joy, but the sense that they are different, as in these drastic metamorphoses, is disturbing, implying that one can't escape time (and death) after all. And yet this series of recognitions has little meaning for Marcel until, as in a mirror, he reads the sign of his old age in the metamorphosed faces around him. The other guests speak to him as to an old man, but he still thinks of himself, just as his mother does, as a child! 'Or je m'apercevais que je me plaçais pour me juger au même point de vue qu'elle' (III, 931): suddenly he sees himself as others see him, but from the very beginning his 'identity' has been in part a kind of mirror-image seen in his mother's eyes.

Marcel has been away from Paris society for some time, but the incredible, grotesque exaggeration which turns everyone's hair white and transforms Marcel himself from a child into an old man, as in the last act of a melodramatic play, seems to divide the span of human life not just into discrete, discontinuous stages ('jeune fille,' 'épaisse matrone,' 'vielle branlante et courbée' (III, 937)) but into two opposing states – childhood and death, the ever-fertile past and the bygone present which life has already passed by. Instead of the long, gradual process of disillusionment which the *Recherche* seems to describe, the structure of a *bildungsroman*, Proust gives us, at the end of his novel, an abrupt passage from one state into another, a final recognition attendant upon a series of revelation-like epiphanies. This rite of passage, postponed from puberty to old age, does not assimilate Marcel into his social group but isolates him from it, transforms him not into a *man* – which, as his mother's eternal child, he never really becomes – but into the alien, borderline figure, endowed with magical powers, of the artist. Indeed, the artist is not simply old and wise: having passed through an ecstatic, visionary transition, he is (in his own mind) already dead.

Marcel claims that he no longer fears physical death. The death of all his past selves, specifically the selves who were in love with a series of lost loves, has prepared him for it: 'Car je comprenais que mourir n'était pas quelque chose de nouveau, mais qu'au contraire depuis mon enfance j'étais déjà mort bien des fois.' (III, 1037-8). But death does threaten the task he still has to accomplish, the writing of his book, and what he calls 'cette crainte raisonnée du danger' (III, 1037) occurs to him when the idea of death itself has become a matter of indifference. It might be more accurate to say that the fear of physical accident – 'la rencontre de l'auto que je prendrais avec un autre' (III, 1037) – has become an irrational, obsessive, almost phobic anxiety about the dangers of being in motion which his newly-acquired magical power over death is designed to dispel. If one accepts the possibility of an accident, the accidental, fortuitous quality of a death that can strike any time, one can enjoy – instead of fear – the rollercoaster-like thrill of physical motion. This is how Marcel feels when he leaves the restaurant at Rivebelle half-drunk and blithely races through the darkness in a carriage (III, 1036). But, as is always the case with Marcel, anxiety and pleasure are inextricably combined: the danger of the carriage ride is the source of his pleasure and the fear that secretly haunts Marcel is not just the fear of death, of physical danger, but of enjoying himself too much, of being overwhelmed by his own desires. The high-speed ride in Dr Percepied's carriage makes Marcel feel that he is being thrown against the Martinville church, but the feeling of controlled anxiety exhilarates him.

The momentous recollections of *Le Temps retrouvé* emerge out of a similar sense of disorientation and disequilibrium, of barely averted danger:

> j'étais entré dans la cour de l'hôtel de Guermantes, et dans ma distraction je n'avais pas vu une voiture qui s'avançait; au cri du wattman je n'eus que le temps de me ranger vivement de côté, et je reculai assez pour buter malgré moi contre les pavés assez mal équarris derrière lesquels était une remise (III, 866).

The momentary loss of equilibrium that Marcel experiences when he puts his foot 'sur un pavé qui était un peu moins élevé que le précédent' (III, 866), the slight swaying motion, is only a miniature, more subtle version of the dizzying sense of 'letting go' he feels when cars or carriages threaten to go out of control. It is not 'accidental' – in the psychological economy of Proust's novel – that Albertine dies as a result of a completely unexpected, fortuitous riding accident, exactly what Marcel himself fears. The danger is ascribed to nonhuman agents – horses, cars, horse-drawn carriages – with the implication that the rational, self-controlled human ego may be swept away and annihilated at any time by the irrational forces of the universe, blind chance.

The 'hululements' of trains do not frighten Marcel only because he knows that 'ces beuglements émanaient de machines reglées'

(III, 880-1 note), under human control. The train in the second 'reminiscence' is not moving, but the very thought of a trainride, to Balbec or Venice, excites Marcel with a pleasure that is almost too much to bear, the imminent satisfaction of his desires making him so upset that he gets sick and can't go. Of course the desire for travel cannot be reduced to the physical sensation of riding in a train, but the idea of seeing something new, something he has only imagined, is itself so disorienting, such a break with sedentary habit, that it seems almost physical. After all, when Marcel wakes up and attempts to remember where he is, the walls seemingly 'tourbill-onnaient dans les ténèbres' (I, 6) and the pieces of furniture only gradually return to their rightful places (I, 187). Mar-cel's symptomatic fear of motion is only a more literal case of his underlying fear of change, a kind of inertial principle carried to an extreme by his invalid aunt Léonie, who never leaves her bed.

And yet Marcel longs to abandon himself to a kind of 'free fall' sensation. Fascinated by these new-fangled machines, cars and airplanes, he experiences perfect, free flight only by leaving the physical world and soaring (like Joyce's Icarus) through the pure ether of the imagination. The cab that takes him to the Guermantes' *matinée* seems to glide effortlessly over the streets, overcoming all external obstacles, simply because these streets near the Champs Elysées are so familiar to him that he doesn't have to bother thinking about them: 'Et, comme un aviateur qui a jusque-là péniblement roulé à terre, "décollant" brusquement, je m'élevais lentement vers les hauteurs silencieuses du souvenir' (III, 858). This effortless soaring prepares us for the ecstatic triumph of the resurrections, where Marcel also escapes from the external world into an inner world of memory, but for the most part (like the 'giants' of the novel's last sentence) Marcel has one foot in the past and one in the present: instead of soaring above the earth, he stumbles.

According to Proust's various spatial metaphors for time, a man carries his past inside him or drags it along behind him (III, 1046-7) – or else this literal span of years is not behind him but beneath him, as if the process of growing older were a never-ending process of growing *up* and up and up. Perched on the 'sommet vertigineux' of time, analogous to those silent heights of memory, Marcel is seized by 'le vertige' that any change, any disorientation, seems to induce in him, and the Duc de Guermantes likewise 'avait vacillé sur des jambes flageolantes...sur le sommet peu praticable de quatre-vingt-trois années' (III, 1047-8). Instead of 'taking off' in an airplane, ageing, mortal men find the gap between their past and present selves growing larger and find themselves walking on stilts, 'sur de vivantes échasses, grandissant sans cesse, parfois plus hautes que des clochers, finissant par leur rendre la marche difficile et périlleuse, et d'où tout d'un coup ils tombaient' (III, 1048). The fear of heights that this image seems to imply is, paradoxically, one of the sources of the aesthetic (sublime) pleasure Marcel feels at the actual sight of lofty, soaring Gothic steeples. Whatever the dangers of horses, cars, trains, carriages, and airplanes, in this last image walking itself becomes precarious, as if the unstable, unreliable machine that one could not be sure of controlling were simply one's own body, as if the doddering (tottering) old man on stilts were really a little child just learning how to walk.[3] The loss of balance, the feeling of giddiness and vertigo that Proust invokes again and again reflects a childlike uncertainty about the physical world one can't control, but this uncertainty makes aesthetic pleasure – the sudden fusion of past and present, of imagination and reality – possible. In tripping on the paving-stones Marcel 'heurte sans le savoir' (III, 866) on the metaphorical door that he's been looking for, reminding us of all the literal doors, windows, and partitions that separate Marcel from the quasi-primal scenes that he eagerly wishes to see. Soon, like Bergotte before his death, he literally stumbles, three times, down the stairs (III, 1039), after which – hardly able to walk – he considers himself 'un demi-mort' (III, 1042).

But images of death and birth go hand in hand in the closing pages of the *Recherche*. When Marcel sees young Mme de Saint-Euverte, the great-niece (by marriage) of old Mme de Saint-Euverte, reclining on a *chaise longue* and wearing a brilliant red-silk Empire dress covered with red fuchsias, she appears to him to be giving birth to a new flowering of the name of Saint-Euverte and the Empire style. Proust often invites us to take his metaphors literally – like the pregnancy of aunt Léonie's kitchen-maid (Giotto's 'Charity'), which, despite its possible allegorical meaning, has to be taken literally (I, 81) – and here, because of her languorous, supine pose, Mme de Saint-Euverte, like aunt Léonie's kitchen-maid, appears to be either ill or pregnant: 'à cause d'une maladie d'estomac, de nerfs, d'une phlébite, d'un accouchement prochain, récent ou manqué'

(III, 1025). That is, her illness may well be the pregnancy she is suffering or recovering from, an identification made still clearer in the possibility of miscarriage, and the fatal illness that Marcel seems to be suffering from will also turn out to be a kind of pregnancy. According to the allegorical interpretation Marcel gives the young woman's pregnancy, the child that she is carrying inside her or cradling in her arms is Time itself, much as the present moment may bear within it (waiting to be reborn) memories of the past. Just as the pink hawthorns of Combray, whose blossoms disclose a blood-red stain, are associated with Gilberte's budding sexuality, the deep-red flowers of Mme de Saint-Euverte's dress represent the full flowering of pregnancy and birth.

At the Guermantes' *matinée* Marcel, despite the recognition that he is growing old, asks Gilberte to introduce him to young girls, and she complies by producing her sixteen-year-old daughter, Odette's granddaughter, the final incarnation in a long series of adolescent *jeunes filles en fleurs*. Because of her parentage, this girl (Mlle de Saint-Loup) seems to represent the intersection of 'Swann's way' and the Guermantes way, in fact of all the various threads of Marcel's past life. Representing his own youth, she seems to embody Time itself. But if she is a mirror-image of the artist as a young man – 'pleine encore d'espérances, riante, formée des années même que j'avais perdues, elle ressemblait à ma Jeunesse' (III, 1032) – the artist himself may leave his virginal self behind and be metamorphosed into the image of that other young girl, that alternative image of female sexuality, Mme de Saint-Euverte, who (like the mother that he finally would like to be) gives birth to Time.

The process of writing a book that truly captures and illuminates life is difficult, laborious, painful, and ultimately fatal: as Marcel puts it in a famous catalogue of comparisons, the writer has to 'préparer son livre minutieusement... le supporter comme une fatigue, l'accepter comme une règle, le construire comme une église, le suivre comme un régime, le vaincre comme un obstacle, le conquérir comme une amitié, le suralimenter comme un enfant' (III, 1032). The writer feeds his book (like a mother a child), but as a result the book 'grandit' and the writer dies, as if children (especially unborn children in the womb) were parasites who sucked the life out of their mothers' bodies, as if motherhood itself were a fatal disease. Wishing, when he was a child, to control his mother's comings and goings, hoping to incorporate her often-absent presence into himself,

Marcel now adopts her magical powers as his own and imagines himself to be this artist-mother who gives birth to a work of art. But in so doing he becomes like a sick, dying mother – like his own self-sacrificing grandmother – who devotes her few remaining days to her son, his work becoming 'comme un fils dont la mère mourante doit encore s'imposer la fatigue de s'occuper sans cesse, entre les piqûres et les ventouses' (III, 1041-2). No longer content to be the melancholy, 'neurasthenic,' asthmatic son or even the invalid aunt whom he comes to resemble, he becomes instead the dying mother (grandmother) who suffers a stroke, who does not need to be loved because she has so much love to give. In his metamorphosis into this selfless, devoted mother, Marcel also comes to identify himself with his devoted servant Françoise, though she too is now old and near-blind. Pinning extra pages to his notebook, his *paperoles* as Françoise calls them – as Proust himself did under the watchful eye of his housekeeper Celeste Albaret – Marcel constructs his book not only like a cathedral 'mais tout simplement comme un robe' (III, 1033), as Françoise herself would have done.

But then the torn pages of Marcel's notebooks seem, to Françoise, like pieces of moth-eaten clothing, for it is time, physical disintegration, approaching death which appears as the enemy of Marcel's work. After the mysterious attack in which he stumbles three times on the stairs, he feels that he no longer has 'ni mémoire, ni pensée, ni force, ni aucune existence.... Je n'avais à proprement parler aucune maladie, mais je sentais que je n'étais plus capable de rien' (III, 1039). Fearing the aphasia that has stricken M. de Charlus as well as his grandmother, he attempts to turn from speaking to the private, solitary, silent practice of writing. But a rigid sense of social obligation – whereby 'la mort ou une grave maladie sont les seules excuses à ne pas venir' to a dinner-party (III, 1040) – compels him to write trivial little notes instead of his novel, excuses for an invitation that he can't accept and condolences on the death of a son! His increasing loss of memory – aphasia gives way to a more general amnesia – helps to free him from these mundane demands, but it also makes him forget the real task in front of him. And yet Marcel *can't* forget his work because it is inside him, germinating, gestating, like the idea of death itself, which never leaves him – the only difference being that, instead of him being delivered of his burden, expelling the foreign invader, it may wind up expelling him. Without this death, there can be no birth, but if he dies to the world, sleeping by day and working by night, as Proust himself did, he 'will bring forth much fruit' (III, 1044).

In short, it is the death of the artist which makes the birth of his work possible; in the process of giving birth, the artist dies. One may object that he merely 'dies to the world,' withdrawing from public, social life, like Proust in his corklined room, not succumbing to time but escaping from it into the extratemporal world of the imagination. But the idea of death, which in fact has kept him company all his life, has a special attraction for Marcel: he welcomes the idea of becoming an artist, of devoting his life to his art, despite the exhausting effort it will entail, because then he will no longer have to bother to live. Being an artist means, in part, that he can retreat into his imagination, relive his past, and never have to do anything else again. If he is already dead, life can no longer hurt him, and he may attain (at least in theory) the perfect serenity of nonexistence. When Marcel, finding his mother's presence as much of a problem as her absence, asks her to leave him alone again, he adds a third phase to the alternation of absence and presence, separation and attachment. This third phase resembles the first (his mother's absence) but the difference is that like the child in the *fort/da* game who pretends that he has his mother on a string, he is now in charge of a situation where he was formerly the helpless victim.[4] So too, in his theory of artistic creation, Marcel renews his self-control and masters his chronic separation-anxiety by playing the role of the *mother* and sending the *son* (the work of art) away, like the child in Freud's example who hides from his image in a mirror, making his own mirror-image disappear, as if 'playing dead.'

II

Joyce's myth of artistic creation is surprisingly similar to Proust's. In *A Portrait of the Artist* Stephen, thinking of his mythical ancestor Daedalus, imagines the artist 'forging anew in his workshop out of the sluggish matter of the earth a new soaring impalpable imperishable being' (P 169). In one sense this ethereal, immortal being is himself, the image of the Daedalian father in his son Icarus. Deciding to become an artist, Stephen imagines himself – or rather, his soul – 'arisen from the grave of boyhood, spurning her graveclothes' (P 170). This rebirth may mark the transition from boyhood to manhood, but Stephen divides himself into the boy that dies and the girlish soul (who used to 'queen it in faded cerements') that lives on. Seeking to embrace both life and art, Stephen becomes not simply a man but an artist, and the 'soul' of the artist is female. The birdlike girl on the beach, an image of sensual life transformed into beautiful art, is also an idealized image of his new artist-self, the beautiful, girlish, birdlike being that can soar above the earth. To create art is, for Stephen, 'to recreate life out of life' (P 172), and the life that is created – projected into the work of art – is his own. If the artist, 'like the God of the creation, remains . . . invisible, refined out of existence' (P 215), it is because he has poured his whole life into his art, controlling everything from a safe, distant, hidden vantage-point, seemingly outside of life. The invisible, ghostly artist is, in a sense, dead: as in Proust, the artist dies, the work of art lives on. Stephen, too, thinks of inspiration as impregnation, or at least as a parody of the immaculate conception: 'O! In the virgin womb of the imagination the word was made flesh' (P 217). The poet (namely Stephen) who writes a villanelle about a virgin temptress wishes not only to surrender himself to her but to be like her: he is tempted, he falls, he gives birth to beautiful language, but miraculously he remains a virgin. In Stephen's unstated theory of 'artistic conception, artistic gestation and artistic reproduction' (P 209), as in Marcel's, the artist is a mother who 'dies' so that the work of art may be born.

Of course it is fatherhood, not motherhood, which is Joyce's essential metaphor for artistic creation. At the end of *A Portrait* Stephen appeals not to a motherly muse but to the 'old father, old artificer' (P 253) Daedalus, the presiding genius of the imagination, and in *Ulysses* he identifies Shakespeare not with Hamlet but with Hamlet's father. Stephen's Shakespeare is, like Daedalus, a totemis-tic ancestor, 'not the father of his own son merely but . . . the father of all his race' (U 208). And yet, if the artist is a Godlike creator, like the 'playwright who wrote the folio of this world,' in the self-sufficient economy of the imagination 'there are no more marriages, glorified man, an androgynous angel, being a wife unto himself' (U 213). Like Zeus giving birth to Pallas Athena out of his own head, the playwright is an androgynous mother-in-the-form-of-a-father who conceives a play in the 'virgin womb' of his imagi-nation and gives birth to it: 'Wait,' says Mulligan, anticipating Bloom's maternal fantasy in 'Circe.' 'I am big with child. I have an unborn child in my brain. Pallas Athena! A play! The play's the thing! Let me parturiate!' (U 208). In *Finnegans Wake* as well, the artist is finally an androgynous parent, a father who plays the part of a mother, like Jarl van Hoother, who gives birth to the 'first piece of poetry in the world' and beats the prankquean at her own game.

In the work of D. H. Lawrence, a neo-Romantic among the modernists, there is no program of aesthetic detachment, no self-conscious myth of artistic creation. As a result, the problems of separation and fusion, of autonomy and dependence, seem even more dangerously insoluble. In *Sons and Lovers* Paul, like Marcel in Proust's *Recherche,* comes to feel that life is meaningless and empty: 'Everything seemed so different, so unreal . . . .There seemed no reason why these things should occupy the space, instead of leaving it empty.' Having lost confidence in the external reality that we normally take for granted, Paul imagines himself as a void within a great universal void, 'at the core a nothingness.' Sexual relations also produce a swooning lapse of consciousness, a temporary loss of self, in which the participants feel like 'blind agents of a great force,' but it is this passive surrender to blind, impersonal forces that is so satisfying. It is not the excitement of passion which appeals to Paul but the relaxation of tension, the 'strange, gentle reaching-out to death,' a kind of 'curious sleep.' These brief, ephemeral moments of Lawrentian fulfillment – of the Lawrentian sublime – depend on the absorption of the self into an all-pervading, all-powerful 'otherness': 'night, and death, and stillness, and inaction, this seemed like *being*. To be alive, to be urgent and insistent – that was *not-to-be*. The highest of all was to melt out into the darkness and sway there, identified with the great Being.'[5] Paul fears the demands that other people (especially women) seem to make on him, and yet he abandons himself to the vast impersonal forces of the universe. The problems of daily life, of actual personal relations, are both too boring and too difficult, and so Paul wishes to escape into an ecstatic state of free-floating fusion where all boundaries collapse and the distinction between being and nothingness no longer applies.

In *Women in Love* Birkin insists upon separateness and independence, renouncing 'the horrible merging, mingling self-abnegation of love' and seeking instead a conjunction of 'two pure beings, each constituting the freedom of the other, balancing each other, like two poles of one force, like two angels, or two demons.' He mistrusts the demands and desires of individual women, but even more he mistrusts 'Woman, the Great Mother of everything out of whom proceeded everything and to whom everything must finally be rendered up.' In his fear of being overwhelmed by an all-powerful mother, he imagines birth in terms of a curiously ambiguous fantasy of castration: 'Always a man must be considered as the broken-off fragment of a woman, and the sex was the still aching scar of the laceration. Man must be added on to a woman, before he had any real place or wholeness.' In this fantasy, which he denies, man (born from a woman) is himself a phallic fragment broken off from a once-phallic mother, and the aching scar of the castration is the sex of (presumably) the woman: after the separation, both fragmented man and scarred woman are seen as 'castrated,' and only their reunion can make them (especially the man) whole again.

Birkin disowns this point of view, because it conflicts with his professed desire for independence, but (like Paul in *Sons and Lovers*) he equates the ultimate goal of love with a sleep that is like death and a death that is like sleep:

I *do* want to die from this life – and yet it is more than life itself. One is delivered over like a naked infant from the womb, all the old defences, and the old body gone, and new air around one, that has never been breathed before.

Even Ursula, Birkin's insufficiently 'polarized' lover, looks forward to 'the pure inhuman otherness of death': 'There one would wash off all the lies and ignominy and dirt that had been put upon one here, a perfect bath of cleanness and glad refreshment, and go unknown, unquestioned, unabased.'[6] Lawrence is borrowing the powerful Biblical rhetoric of redemption and rebirth, of dying into a new life, but this rhetoric is so moving, so effective, because it implies that death is only a return to a peaceful, sleepy womb followed by a new birth into uncontaminated childhood innocence. In the womb and as an infant, at least in this fantasy, one is free to live one's own life as one pleases – but always in the total security provided by an all-protecting mother. So Birkin mistrusts women and detests the 'Great Mother,' but he is willing to surrender his life to the 'pure inhuman otherness of death,' to the apparently impersonal, inhuman force 'to whom everything must finally be rendered up' – in short, to the mythical projection of a personal, human mother, the Great Mother 'out of whom proceeded everything.' He fears what he most desires, and his desire for personal autonomy and self-control is outweighed only by a more deep-seated desire to abandon self-control, lose consciousness, and merge with the quasi-maternal cosmic forces of 'Being.'

Despite Lawrence's later disagreements with Freud, *Sons and Lovers* has often been read as a Freudian, 'oedipal' novel about a son who loves his mother too much – and resents the father who is a rival for his mother's love. But Lawrence ascribes the origin of these 'oedipal' sentiments to the mother as much as to the son, to the early 'symbiotic' relationship between them as much as to later sexual desires, and the son's feelings toward *both* his parents grow increasingly confused and ambivalent. In one powerful, noteworthy scene, near the end of the book, when his mother is dying of cancer, Paul 'conspires' with his sister to end her suffering by poisoning her milk with an overdose of morphia: thus doubly reversing the infantile oral relation of a mother feeding her child, poisoning her instead of nourishing her, in an effort to let her die in peace, to end his dependence on her, and perhaps (as the final pages of the book imply) to merge with her at last on some cosmic, disembodied level. Beyond or beneath the classic oedipal triangle there is a deep-seated preoedipal ambivalence between the need for a mother's love and the need to be independent and autonomous. The Oedipus complex – particularly the rivalry between sons and fathers – became the cornerstone of Freud's theory of sexuality, and only gradually did he come to recognize the importance of the mother's 'preoedipal' role as the first source and 'object' of love. The so-called 'negative' Oedipus complex, in which the male child identifies himself with his mother and attempts to appease his father, does not adequately explain the original 'symbiotic' relationship, close identification, and inevitable ambivalence between any child – male or female – and its mother.[7]

Freud's discovery of the Oedipus complex as an underlying structure of the human family marked a turning-point, a revolution, in our understanding of sexual desire, psychological conflict, and the relations between parents and children. And though this structure is most appropriate to the typical middle-class, middle-European family of the late nineteenth century, with its dominant father (both inside and outside the home) and its housebound, childbearing mother, it is nonetheless potentially relevant in its application to all family structures that develop out of the biological characteristics of the human species – the need for two parents, of opposite sex, to create (conceive) the child, the need for the relatively helpless infant to be taken care of, both physically and emotionally, by *someone,* whether a biological mother, a father, a substitute for these parents, an extended family of parents, uncles, and grandparents, or any cooperative or collective group of amateur or professional childcare workers. If the Western nuclear family of the last few centuries is replaced, in other cultures, by matrilineal kinship structures in which the maternal uncle takes over many of the functions of the biological father, or in our own, by less patriarchal structures in which the father takes over many of the 'traditional' functions of the mother and both parents are less authoritarian, less 'repressive,' if the family becomes smaller (fewer children) or the social group in which even children play a role becomes larger, then undoubtedly the oedipal pattern of desire, conflict, and ambivalence will show significant changes. But it will not simply disappear, as long as there are two sexes (not necessarily present), a need (not necessarily fulfilled) for a 'symbiotic,' nurturing relationship in the first months and years of life, and the inevitable fact that adults exercise authority over children, do not grant them all the wishes that they ask for, and cannot gratify all their desires even if they want to. In short, the oedipal pattern might be broadened to include all variations in family structure and might be extended to mean all conflicts between desire and authority in a child's relations with his/her parents or 'parents.'[8]

But this is not enough: the infant's 'symbiotic,' preoedipal relationship with what is usually a mother – inherently unstable, always tinged by anxiety – lays the foundation not only for his/her future relations with others but for his/her own fundamental sense of 'self.' And the problem of establishing one's identity – even one's 'sexual identity,' one's sense of being male or female – depends largely on one's identifications with parental figures, including one's earliest, ambivalent identification with one's mother. These early identifications seem more important for the creation of a 'sexual identity' than the specific anatomical 'castration anxiety' that Freud locates at the heart of the Oedipus complex, despite the importance of phallic symbolism for boys and, to a lesser extent, for girls.[9] In this light we should compare girls' fantasies of possessing a penis (the notorious 'penis envy,' and its corollary that 'anatomy is destiny') with boys' fantasies of giving birth to children: indeed, children's fantasies of how babies are born – with or without the intervention of a penis, from this or that anatomical opening, with or without the assistance of a 'phallic mother' – obviously cross sexual lines and are not limited to real possibilities. Moreover, men's fascination with the mysteries of childbirth and menstruation (and the bleeding that may accompany a virgin's first sexual relations) is an ancient and widespread cultural phenomenon.[10] In short, 'sexual identity' is not simply a biological given nor simply a consequence of a preformed (instinctual) oedipal pattern, with room for pathological variations. The specific interpersonal relations between the child and its parents play a major role, and – to be more specific – the original, preoedipal dependence of a male child on his mother affects not only his future sense of identity but his sense of being male.[11] Surely maternal deprivation may have an effect, but so also may the kind of exaggerated, prolonged 'overprotection,' the refusal to allow the child necessary freedom and autonomy, that Lawrence implies in *Sons and Lovers*. Is this what happens in Proust's *Recherche*, or is this only what Marcel would like to happen?

Even in the Oedipus myth, the hero who unwittingly kills his father also symbolically 'slays' a dangerous, uncanny, monstrous female figure – the sphinx – by solving her riddle (with its phallic overtones) and so 'stealing' from her the secret knowledge of what it is to be a man, a feat of ratiocination which he tries to perform again when he attempts to discover the cause of the plague, solve the murder of Laius, and uncover the truth about his own origins. Thus Oedipus is, among other things, a culture-hero who steals the knowledge of what it is to be male (namely, possessing three 'legs,' where the third leg is not a walking stick but a penis) from the creature who apparently knows the answer to such questions better than any man, a powerful, inscrutable, deadly 'mother.' Indeed, if this primitive, archaic legend – of male rationality overcoming a dangerous female monster – raises questions about the central Oedipus myth, we might do well to shift our attention from Sophocles' play to *The Bacchae* of Euripides, whose central problem is the god-inspired madness of women.

Dionysus, who is called 'twice-born,' claims to have been born first from his mother Semele and then from his father Zeus, whose thigh conceals a 'secret womb.'[12] This story is meant to vindicate Semele, to prove that she did not surrender her virginity to any mortal man, that Dionysus is both a 'legitimate' son and a divine one – like Jesus Christ, another messianic leader of a religious cult who claims to be the son of a divine father and a virgin mother. It also transfers a woman's childbearing power to a male god. Indeed, Semele dies in childbirth, as if punished for her sin – killed by the lightning flash of divine (but also male) power – and Dionysus punishes Semele's sisters, who questioned her 'honor,' by driving them mad, turning them into Maenads (Bacchantes). In effect, Dionysus restores his own mother's virginity by turning other women – including the mother of his cousin Pentheus – into hysterical, sex-crazed monsters, fatal to behold.

In the end the Maenads uproot the high, quasi-phallic tree on which Pentheus is perched and, led by his mother Agave, who is not in her right mind, tear him limb from limb. Pentheus, the all-too-human alter ego of his cousin Dionysus, is the (Christlike) scapegoat-victim of the Dionysian totem feast – Agave wants to eat the beast she's just killed – but in this version the man dies while the god (who is already 'reborn') lives on. As we can see, the Dionysian myth is radically different from Freud's myth, in *Totem and Taboo,* of sons banding together to kill a father. The women kill – behead, dismember, 'castrate' – a man, but in so doing they seem to be exchanging a woman's traditional role for a man's. As Agave says, 'I have left weaving at the loom for greater things,/For hunting wild beasts with my bare hands.' Besides, this power is not their own: it comes from the divine frenzy instilled in them by the male god Dionysus, by whom they are 'possessed.' The uncertain division between male and female is evident in Dionysus himself, a young, powerful, masculine god who drives women wild, but who has long flowing hair and appears 'effeminate.'[13] In fact, under the magical, supernatural influence of Dionysus, Pentheus, the prurient, repressive hypocrite who wants to spy on the women he condemns, who envies their special, secret power, dresses up like a woman so that he won't be noticed!

In short, the play repeatedly reverses the roles and powers traditionally ascribed to men and women. The 'traditional' irrationality of women is transformed – through the divine madness instilled in them by an ambiguously androgynous god – into the violent, aggressive power usually associated with men. And Zeus, the powerful 'father' of the gods, appears as an androgynous, childbearing 'mother' who gives birth to his own child out of his own womb, like Joyce's Jarl van Hoother in his mythlike tale of the prankquean. The divine son, the powerful leader of a cult of female followers, has an 'effeminate' appearance, and his human counterpart Pentheus, jealous of women, jealous of Dionysus, plays the part of a transvestite. And if, according to the magical-symbolic logic of the myth, the women assimilate the supernatural *mana* of the wine-god by drinking wine, taking possession of the power by which they are themselves 'possessed,' in this play a mother almost carries out the ritual incorporation of the totem feast on her own son, killing, dismembering, and almost eating him: as if to imply that a man's deepest fear is the infantile oral one of being swallowed up by his mother. Over and over again the play reveals the profoundly ambivalent, contradictory attitude of men toward women, a deep-seated fear and envy of the mysterious, uncanny powers that women – especially mothers – seem to possess.[14]

As I have been arguing, the original, preoedipal dependence of a child on its mother creates intense, ambivalent feelings that may not ever be fully outgrown. This bewildering compound of overwhelming need and hostile resentment appears prominently in Proust's work: from the early *Confession d'une jeune fille*, about a girl who 'betrays' her mother, provokes her death, and then decides to commit suicide, and the so-called 'Sentiments filiaux d'un parricide,' about the actual case of a man who kills his mother and then himself, to the *Recherche* itself, where Mlle Vinteuil hastens the death of her devoted, 'motherly' father, Berma's daughter and son-in-law do the same to her, and Marcel himself claims to feel guilty over what he calls the 'double murder' of his mistress Albertine and his 'doubly' maternal grandmother. After his grandmother's death Marcel punishes himself, with an almost masochistic fervor, for the 'grief' he has caused her, but grief, 'melancholia,' seems to have been Marcel's natural condition, as if he were always in mourning for the mother who might, at any time, leave him.[15] Indeed, the whole *Recherche* may be seen as Marcel's attempt to free himself from his mother and create an independent existence for himself, a long-delayed process of growing up which begins when Marcel 'forces' his mother to stay the night with him, feels guilty about it, and wishes she would leave him in peace. His final resolution of the problem is, as we have noted, a kind of suicidal self-punishment in which he takes his *grand*mother's suffering upon himself, as she had taken his upon her: 'Ma grand'mère que j'avais, avec tant d'indifférence, vue agoniser et mourir près de moi! O puissé-je, en expiation, quand mon oeuvre serait terminée, blessé sans remède, souffrir de longues heures, abandonné de tous, avant de mourir!' (III, 902). Marcel's mother takes up Mme de Sévigné and comes to resemble his grandmother, while at the end of the novel Marcel imagines himself as a dying mother who gives his (her) life so that a new Marcel may live in the pages of his book. The *jeunes filles en fleurs* of Balbec – not to mention the ambiguously 'androgynous' homosexuals of both sexes that proliferate as the novel progresses, implicating even Albertine – already indicate Marcel's uncertainty about the sexual identity of those he loves. But in the end Marcel imagines himself in a quasi-feminine role: detaching himself from his mother at last, he also identifies himself with her, merges with her, and adopts her self-sacrificing, child-nurturing role. And yet – no longer alive, giving birth to a new 'child' that will take his place – he is no longer himself.

If Stephen Dedalus (in Joyce's *Ulysses*) tries to prove that Shakespeare is the father of himself, like God in certain versions of the Trinity, Proust's myth of artistic creation reflects an even deeper, more fundamental desire to be one's own mother, thereby overcoming one's dependence and becoming fully autonomous and self-sufficient at last. Marcel implicitly believes that the magical, creative power – the *mana* or essence – which animates the universe and may give 'life' to art originates in a mother. In order to become an artist, he appropriates that creative, life-giving power and becomes – symbolically – a mother, This 'mythical,' symbolic solution to the reciprocal problems of separation and attachment, of dependence and autonomy, is certainly magical, irrational, and 'fantasmatic,' like Joyce's more comic fantasies of androgynous parents: how then is it different from Lawrence's self-contradictory, apocalyptic, quasi-mystical, and potentially authoritarian 'solutions' to what, after all, are similar problems? Doesn't art inevitably offer imaginary solutions – or rather magical and symbolic ones – to real problems?

To begin with, though we never know how literally to take Lawrence's mystical, apocalyptic rhetoric of death and rebirth, Proust's analogy of a dying mother sacrificing herself for her child is more clearly metaphorical and symbolic: expressed in extended similes ('comme un fils dont la mère mourante,' 'le suralimenter comme un enfant'), reinforced by the double-edged pregnancy-like image of death taking up residence inside Marcel, and 'physically' represented in the image (observed by Marcel) of the pregnant-

appearing Mme de Saint-Euverte. Though Marcel matches Lawrence's Biblical rhetoric with his homily about the grain of wheat
needing to die in order to bring forth much fruit, he seems to have
survived his stroke-like attack, his near-fall on the stairs, and the
half-dead condition in which it leaves him – and written his
voluminous novel after all. His mysterious attack, his ambiguous
condition, and the idea of a death that will bring forth life remain
suspiciously 'symbolic' elements of a personal, self-created
myth – not (as in Lawrence's work) what appear to be the mystical
revelations of a newly discovered religion, whose prophet is Lawrence himself. But this is unfair to Lawrence: we might as well
criticize Blake for being a visionary. More significantly, instead of
Lawrence's 'valorization' of death as a cosmic fusion in which one
loses consciousness, loses one's sense of self, and merges with the
forces of the universe, Proust's symbolization of death implies *both*
fusion and detachment, both gratification and suffering, both an
escape from everyday life and a reassertion of conscious, rational
control, both the loss of self and the creation of a new, stronger
identity (the artist). Moreover, in contrast to the apocalyptic fusions
of the Lawrentian 'sublime,' the deathlike detachment that Marcel
invokes begins with the initial 'impregnation' of a specific impression, the 'sublime' but ephemeral interpenetration of inner and
outer worlds, which gives him the insight that enables him to
undertake the difficult, exhausting, painful, and allegedly 'fatal' task
of writing a novel. In short, Proust's symbolic scenario of artistic
inspiration and artistic creation maintains a complex and delicately
balanced equilibrium between the competing claims of separation
and attachment, between the desire to be self-sufficient, self-
sustaining, self-creating and the need to be part of a 'real' – natural,
social – world.

The hope of avoiding all change that threatens to turn Marcel
into another aunt Léonie, the longing for death that, in one way or
another, infects the work of Proust, Joyce, Lawrence, Kafka,
Beckett, and many other modern writers, necessarily reminds us of
the Freudian death instinct, the entropy-like drive that Freud
hypothesized in order to explain the apparently irrational need to
repeat painful experiences, exemplified by the little child's *fort/da*,
hide-and-seek game in *Beyond the Pleasure Principle*. Indeed, the very
problem of repetition recurs in Freudian thought in numerous
forms: from the early explanation of hysteria as the 'reminiscence'

of some buried memory, the theory of repression implying an inevitable 'return of the repressed,' and the analysis of the 'uncanny' as a kind of *déjà vu*, to the 'repetition compulsion' itself. Proust's own 'search for lost time,' an attempt to cross the gap between present and past, reveals this structure of recurrence in the spontaneous return of unconscious memories, in the guilt-ridden 'intermittences' of grief, and in Marcel's own need to repeat and recover the past. In fact, the cyclical structure of the narrative – the division of the self into the hero who grows up and the narrator who reconstructs his own past history – is an elaborate attempt to reverse the authority of the past over the present, to overcome past anxieties by 'replaying' them under new ground rules.

But the internal entropy-principle that seems to govern Marcel's life – that leads to a symbolic suicide for the sake of art – is not a death instinct, genetically programmed, a 'law of nature' like the laws of thermodynamics. On the contrary, it is a defensive strategy that grows out of a child's earliest experiences of 'symbiosis' and separation, and it reflects an attempt to avoid the anxiety that these experiences create. Marcel, though he withdraws from the world, devotes himself to his art, and seems finally to be dying rather than living – very much like Proust in his overheated, airless, corklined room, sleeping by day and working by night – is not aunt Léonie, who refuses to be 'violated' by life. He is, rather, a 'mother' who gives birth, and if he were not in some sense willing to be 'impregnated' by that dangerous foreign substance – life – which frightens him so much, he would never be a writer. Of course this is a symbolic, even magical solution to the problem of becoming an artist, a self-created myth of self-creation: as Marcel's own emphasis on 'decipherment' reminds us, the symbolic figure of the artist dying in the process of giving birth to a work of art is not simply a myth to be believed in but a sign that has to be read and interpreted. It is just this opposition between art and life, between imagination and reality, between inner and outer worlds, that Proust's text attempts to overcome: not by turning 'reality' into a purely subjective, ideal realm but by revealing that the relations that govern the self – the structures in which it is 'inscribed' – are inescapably symbolic.

7 Theoretical conclusion: psycho-analysis, literary theory, and recent Proust criticism

In the wake of what I have called a psychoanalytic interpretation of Proust's novel, we should remind ourselves of the profound theoretical problems inherent in any attempt to 'interpret' or even 'analyze' a literary work. These problems affect literary criticism in general, where varieties of structuralist and semiological thinking, based on Saussurean linguistics, have undermined traditional assumptions about meaning and content in literary works. But it is especially true of psychoanalytic criticism, where a 'new psychoanalysis' has arisen, based on the 'structural' psychoanalysis of Jacques Lacan, for whom 'the unconscious is structured like a language,' but also on the rigorously 'deconstructionist' approach of Jacques Derrida. Lacan's emphasis on linguistic relations (such as metaphor and metonymy) as models for psychological processes, his analysis of interpersonal relations in terms of symbolic structures, and his insistence upon the verbal/symbolic dimension of psychoanalytic theory (and practice) make the new, French version of Freud seem particularly relevant to questions of literary analysis.[1] Derrida, in turn, though somewhat ambivalent about psychoanalysis, shatters the surface unity of discourse, exposes the irreconcilable contradictions and inconsistencies in apparently meaningful statements, and brings this quasi-Freudian practice of 'suspicious,' skeptical reading to bear upon Freud's texts themselves.[2]

This deconstructive approach forces one to abandon any vestigial faith in absolute meaning and truth and to trace instead the literal, verbal 'play of signifiers' in which each text reveals its own multiple and contradictory significations. After Derrida, one cannot naively 'use' Freudian theory to interpret a work of literature, because Freud's own writings – like all philosophical texts since Plato and Aristotle – betray (to a greater or lesser degree) the same metaphysical assumptions about the human subject, about consciousness and self-consciousness, about language, truth, reality, and the determinable origins of determinate meanings, that vitiate the literary texts themselves. Or, rather, the literary texts, insofar as they avoid metaphysical assertions and affirm multiplicity, contradiction, and indeterminacy – that is, insofar as we can ignore their metaphysical assertions and accept their indeterminacy, whatever 'they' (or their authors) may seem to say about themselves – may help to expose and deconstruct the 'logocentric' illusion of Western thought, the illusory belief in presence, unity, fixed origins, or final explanations. In this light, the writings of Freud and Mallarmé, Lévi-Strauss and Rousseau, Plato and Artaud, cannot be arranged in any hierarchy of philosophical truth and poetic fiction. This is a false dichotomy which is undermined in every (literary or philosophical, scientific or mythological) text. So far so good. But are Lacan's linguistic models, psychological structures and symbolic exchanges compatible with Derrida's all-engulfing 'grammatology,' which sweeps every text and every discourse (including Freud's, including Lacan's) into an endlessly self-perpetuating and self-deconstructing circulation or 'dissemination' of signs. In short, can we hope (through literary works?) to interpret the symbolic structures of human relations, the symbolic relations of a problematic self, or is every work, every text, and every theoretical statement merely a self-reflecting, self-dissolving commentary upon the arbitrary, differential quality of signs and the impossibility of interpretation? Symbolic structures or an open-ended chain of signifiers? Problematics of the 'self' or language about language? *Or,* if the self is inscribed in (constructed out of) a quasi-linguistic structure of exchanges, and if the linguistic circulation of signs can never be circumscribed by any individual text, then perhaps psychoanalytic interpretation and textual deconstruction are not absolutely incompatible.

Freudian psychoanalysis traditionally claims to discover hidden, unconscious meanings, but in the *Interpretation of Dreams* Freud himself warned against the kind of facile, dogmatic, one-to-one 'decoding' that reduces complex symbolic constructions to so-called 'Freudian symbols' (a warning he did not always heed) and insisted, instead, that each 'dream-symbol' (each signifier) should be read in the overall context of the dream – in fact, in the whole context of the dreamer's associations, memories, responses, and 'explanations.'[3] In short, psychoanalytic interpretation is or ought to be 'contextual.' Michael Sherwood, in his careful, cautious study of *The Logic of*

Explanation in Psychoanalysis, argues from Freud's analysis of the so-called 'rat man' case that any interpretations of dreams, symptoms, obsessional behavior, or what the patient says in the analytic session, must proceed from the entire context of the patient's life-history, [4] although it is never quite clear whether one is seeking the patient's personal reconstruction of his own past – his mythical, symbolic autobiography – or what 'actually' happened to him in his childhood.[5] Let us say, simply, that the interpretation of any particular symbol (that is, signifier) depends upon the entire symbolic structure of which it forms a part. The relevance of psychoanalysis for literary criticism lies less in Freud's 'metapsychological' explanations of human behavior than in his strategy for interpreting symbolic structures, whether they be the quasi-cinematic narratives of dreams, the 'free associations' of a patient in analysis, the specific symptoms of obsession or hysteria, the anonymous, collective formulations of myth and ritual, or even the complex constructions of a literary text. Of course I am referring not simply to Freud's specific interpretations of dreams, case histories or works of literature, but to his general theory of multiple, contradictory meanings, of 'symbolic' substitution, identification, and displacement.

However, in apparent contrast to Freudian strategies of reading, the formalistic, linguistic disposition of structuralist criticism (not to mention the radically deconstructive strategy of Derrida) implies an emphasis on sign and structure rather than signification, on form rather than meaning, on content-free 'analysis' rather than symbolic interpretation. The notion of contextual interpretation (instead of unconscious content) may help to bridge the gap between psychoanalysis and 'structuralism,' and Lacan's notion of 'the symbolic' (based on the models of Saussurean linguistics) seems to offer a structural theory of psychoanalysis. Still, some crucial questions remain: Is there a psychoanalytic theory of interpretation, a specifically psychoanalytic way of interpreting symbolic structures (not simply a specifically psychoanalytic 'content')? And, in the wake of Derrida's decentering, deconstructive critique of all possible meanings, intentions, origins, and explanations, his insistence that reading and writing are endlessly reciprocal processes, isn't the very idea of interpretation itself suspect? There is no easy answer to these questions, but I would like to offer a response to them in the context of recent Proust criticism, since many of these same problems are raised both in Proust's novel itself and in critical responses to that novel.[6] In referring to these critical works, I do not mean to pretend that I am giving an exhaustive analysis of them or that this work has 'superseded' them. But I do wish to suggest how this work differs from previous ones (even as it remains indebted to them) and how my own particular strategy of psychoanalytic interpretation may offer new ways of reading Proust's text.

Traditional novelistic criticism has tried to make clear what the novel itself 'says,' to translate the implicit themes of the novel into more explicit discursive terms. Even when this translation is subtle and complex, the traditional critic has normally ended up trying to demonstrate the overall unity of the work or of the attitudes on the part of the author implied by the work. Proust's novel is particularly tempting to read in this way, since, seeming to interpret itself, it identifies its own major themes, reveals its own messages, and makes explicit statements about art, life, and the relation between the two. Indeed, it is seductively easy to identify the narrator who makes these statements with Proust himself, the author who, having abandoned early illusions and discovered essential truths, presides over and interprets his own novel. Thus the first step in a critical reading of the novel is to resist the identification of the double 'I' of the text (protagonist and narrator) with any final or absolute authorial judgment. (Biographical knowledge of Proust's life can raise more questions but it cannot provide any conclusive answers.) But this is only the first step. Jeffrey Mehlman, claiming that

> literary critics, on the whole, sensing the enormous complexity of the text Proust wrote in the name of (esthetic) values they share, have seen their role as one of rendering explicit the elaborateness with which the author pursued his goals,

quotes Philippe Sollers on reading Proust's text against the grain, between the lines, in opposition to its own self-justifications:

> Lire Proust? Ce serait pratiquer désormais dans la *Recherche* des coupes, des tassements, des blancs, des chocs, des incompatibilités: casser le projet d'ensemble, souligner les points d'aberration mal contrôlés, dégager une logique sous-jacente recouverte par un vernissage de continuité.[7]

Some critics have begun to do this. In contrast to the apparent emphasis, even in the title of *A la Recherche du temps perdu*, on time, memory, and the recovery of what has been lost, several critics have minimized the importance of involuntary memory and have stressed the role of discontinuity, distance, and division in the work. Indeed, Georges Poulet, in a book called *Proustian Space*, discusses the transformation (in Proust's text) of time into space. Citing the passage in which Marcel runs back and forth between two train windows in order to see both 'views' (almost) simultaneously, Poulet contrasts temporal superimposition with spatial juxtaposition.[8] But a later critic, more skeptical of aesthetic unity, criticizes Poulet for concluding that Proustian juxtaposition is 'a multiplicity unified by the active presence of one single actor and one single author.'[9] Gilles Deleuze, in his emphasis on the complex, 'transversal' interrelation of *signs*, seeks to avoid ascribing this sort of idealized aesthetic unity to Proust's work, and his chapter called 'Antilogos' might seem to parallel Derrida's critique of the 'logocentric' faith in final or original truths: 'We are wrong to believe in facts,' writes Deleuze, 'there are only signs. We are wrong to believe in truth; there are only interpretations.' But in his effort to be 'true' to Proust's text, he reaffirms the author's apparent faith in the transcendent unity and truth of spirit, essence, and art: 'art gives us the true unity: unity of an immaterial sign and of an entirely spiritual meaning. The essence is precisely this unity of sign and meaning as it is revealed in the work of art.' And, in an attempt to define 'this very special mode of unity irreducible to any "unification," ' he declares: 'in a world reduced to a multiplicity of chaos, it is only the formal structure of the work of art, insofar as it does not refer to anything else, which can serve as unity – afterwards.'[10] I do not mean to misrepresent Deleuze by quoting him out of context, but it seems clear that, despite his post-Saussurean emphasis on signs, he reinstates the old metaphysical dichotomies between spirit and matter, essence and object, art and life. (The critical questions are: Are these dichotomies 'true' to Proust's text? And in what sense should a work of criticism be 'true' (to a text), particularly if these dichotomies do not constitute the only truth or the only way of representing the problem of truth?) Rightly or wrongly, each critic seems to subsume the multiplicity of Proust's text into a higher unity, and it is just this fatal 'error' – of course 'error' reinstates the truth/error opposition that may be inappropriate to either the fictional or the critical text – that later critics have seized upon in their effort to shatter the apparent unity of the work.

Gérard Genette, in a series of linguistically-oriented articles,[11] has sought to demonstrate that Proust's text, whatever its (apparent) pretensions to unity, truth, and a 'higher' reality, is in itself

> une critique de cette illusion réaliste qui consiste à chercher dans le langage une image fidèle, une expression directe de la réalité: utopie cratylienne (ignorante ou 'poétique') d'une motivation du signe, d'un rapport naturel entre le nom et le lieu, le mot et la chose.

And this text, far from arriving at a final truth or transcendent reality, reveals (in Genette's words)

> le décentrement de la parole, fût-elle la plus 'sincère,' par rapport à la 'vérité' intérieure, et l'incapacité du langage à révéler cette vérité autrement que d'une manière dérobée, déplacée, déguisée, retournée, toujours indirecte et comme seconde: c'est l'*âge des mots.*[12]

In addition, in an article called 'Métonymie chez Proust,' Genette, seeking to rectify the 'overestimation' of metaphor as an explanation of the theory and practice of Proust's text (initiated by the narrator in the text itself), demonstrates the complex interrelation of metaphor and metonymy in individual 'metaphors' and in the narrative as a whole, so that it is the very principle of metonymical continuity (claims Genette) that makes an extended narrative possible: 'Sans métaphore, dit (à peu près) Proust, pas de véritables souvenirs . . . sans métonymie, pas d'enchaînement de souvenirs, pas d'*histoire,* pas de roman.'[13]

Genette's careful, precise studies of linguistic relations would seem to escape the Proustian snares of 'truth' and 'unity,' but Paul de Man asserts that the combination of figural modes, in Genette's article on metonymy, 'is treated descriptively and non-dialectically without suffering the possibility of logical tensions.'[14] And Samuel Weber, after praising Genette for taking 'the first, decisive step' in the attempt to show 'how the declared intention of [Proust's] work is contraverted by its textual practice,' demonstrates, point by point, that Genette's explanations (of the relation between metaphor and metonymy) are based on mistaken or misleading assumptions about the status of the text (any text). When Genette discusses two possible ways of reading, suggesting that it may not be possible to *choose* between them, Weber 'deconstructs' Genette's problematical alternatives:

> the critic, according to Genette, can assume either a position *inside* the text: that of Marcel, and conclude that the metonymy produces the metaphor; *or* he can identify with the narrative itself, and conclude that metonymy is simply a means used to produce the metaphor, its *causa finalis.* The error is to think that this latter point of view, that of the narrative discourse, is *outside* the text, 'devant lui' and not inscribed in it: the 'autobiography' is no less fictional than the 'fictional' situation of Marcel, and the choice is not whether or not to 'rester dans ce tourniquet,' – this is unavoidable – but of how to describe one's position in it.[15]

Indeed, Weber takes *all* previous critics to task (including Genette, Deleuze, and Poulet) for being the faithful 'porte-parole' of the narrative discourse, content to repeat and articulate its implicit intentions and aspirations:

> The entire critical corpus, based on a hermeneutics of penetration and discovery, guided by the notions of truth, essence, spirit, or any other of the Proustian values, fails to take account of the problematic status of the narrative discourse, of which those values are the expression.[16]

Moreover, de Man, in a precise reading of specific passages ('not "our" reading, since it uses only the linguistic elements provided by the text'), undermines (like Genette) the supposed superiority of metaphor over metonymy, exposes the metaphysical assumptions behind this valuation, but also reveals that the interrelation of the two modes is more complex, more problematical than Genette has led us to believe. In fact, de Man's essay on 'Proust et l'allégorie de la lecture' claims that Proust's text is not merely the allegory of its own reading, not merely the narrative of its own deconstruction, but the 'allegorical' narrative of the *impossibility* of reading:

> Tout dans ce roman est signe allégorique et signifie autre chose qu'il ne représente ... On peut montrer que le meilleur terme

pour désigner cette 'autre chose' est: la Lecture. Mais on doit
'comprendre' en même temps que ce mot barre à tout jamais
l'accès à un sens qui ne peut pourtant jamais se résigner à ne pas
être atteint.[17]

The radically deconstructive strategies of both Weber and de Man
appear to show that a literary text can never be completely
'explained' by any structural oppositions (metaphor/metonymy,
literal/figural) brought to bear upon it, because these oppositions
are necessarily undermined and called into question by the text
itself.

Indeed, such oppositions are themselves metaphorical, and de
Man, borrowing the metaphorical opposition of inside and outside
from Proust's text, claims that modern formalist (structuralist)
criticism has reversed the usual terms of criticism without challeng-
ing the essential opposition: 'The polarities of inside and outside
have been reversed, but they are still the same polarities that are at
play: internal meaning has become outside reference and the outer
form has become the intrinsic structure.' It is the desire to reconcile
form and meaning, says de Man, that

> accounts for the metaphorical model of literature as a kind of box
> that separates an inside from an outside, and the reader or critic
> as the person who opens the lid in order to release in the open
> what was secreted but inaccessible inside. It matters little whether
> we call the inside of the box the content or the form, the outside
> the meaning or the appearance. The recurrent debate opposing
> intrinsic to extrinsic criticism stands under the aegis of an
> inside/outside metaphor that is never being seriously ques-
> tioned.[18]

Or, as Weber puts it: 'If the opposition "surface-depth" is thus itself
"superficial," then the critical effort to move beyond the surface
cannot be understood to imply a veritable, essential, and immanent
depth, nor can the surface be simply superficial.'[19]

Where does the Genette–de Man–Weber 'controversy' lead (if not
to any final truth or final meaning)? As we have noted, Roman
Jakobson's influential, widely-adopted distinction between metaphor

and metonymy as two primary linguistic modes (based on similarity and contiguity, respectively) *is itself metaphorical,* translating different kinds of identifications and associations into a sort of binary grammar.[20] The opposition between the two terms is not an absolute division, and perhaps the categories themselves do not have clearly-defined meanings or uses, which may be a source of unrecognized confusion: for example, is it appropriate to identify the idea (or the representation) of spatio-temporal contiguity with the quasi-temporal *verbal* sequence of the narrative? They are both, in our terms, 'metonymical,' but it is a metaphor to say so (the identification is based on a presumed similarity, which should not obscure the differences between the two kinds or 'levels' of signs). Jonathan Culler suggests that metaphor implies two incompatible notions:

> the notion of a definable rhetorical operation in which I say X and mean Y and the open-ended violations of *vraisemblance* through which we are invited to explore, develop, and fill in a space of signification . . . . Literature's power has been thought to lie in metaphor [first definition], but in fact it is precisely literature's resistance to metaphor, resistance to replacement operations, which is the source of this power.[21]

In short, a literary – even a psychoanalytic – theory of metaphor, of figural 'meaning' in general, must move beyond simple, classificatory oppositions (metaphor/metonymy, literal/figural) to a 'contextual' model of repetitions, associations, displacements, substitutions, and identifications in which each signifier is read both in its immediate 'syntagmatic' context and in the overall context of the text as a whole. This is the sense in which I discuss, for example, the metaphorical *relation* between flowers and girls in chapter 4 of this study.

And if, after the powerful cautionary homiletics of de Man and Weber, I still 'employ' (provisionally) the distinction between metaphor and metonymy (in chapter 5), if only to demonstrate once more their interrelation, it is because these terms correspond (one explicitly, the other implicitly) to two antithetical tendencies which are inextricably, inseparably combined in Proust's text. Or, rather, to be more precise: (1) these tendencies remain in a perpetual equilibrium or (if one prefers) disequilibrium in the text, and (2) *each* equilibrium of (if one prefers) disequilibrium in the text, and (2) *each* quasi-linguistic relation 'contains' *both* antithetical tendencies in itself, in a different balance or imbalance. And it is just the inescapable, insoluble 'disequilibrium' of these opposing tendencies, the contradiction between them, that manifests itself in every 'aspect,' on every 'level' (without implying any hierarchy of levels, any surface/depth valorization) of the *Recherche.* This (in one of its forms) is the quasi-metaphorical/quasi-metonymical opposition which Poulet observes between temporal superimposition and spatial juxtaposition. But, despite the text's apparent valorization of a 'metaphorical' idea of temporal 'intermittence,' neither term can be considered as privileged over the other. Moreover, as I demon-strate at greater length in chapter 5, temporal discontinuity also implies (in the work itself) a precarious, unstable 'unity' of separate moments, and spatial contiguity may signify not only the merger of neighboring zones but also the impenetrable, impregnable boun-dary between them. Thus the two antithetical possibilities whose (dis)equilibrium seems to mark the play of signifiers in the text – which *cannot* be explained simply by the opposition of two rhetorical modes – are: merger and separation (or, in more abstract terms, unity and division). But suddenly, in this final formulation, we seem to have arrived precisely at that vague and spurious paradox of a multiple, divided unity which every Proustian critic seems to have substituted for the text itself until (so it appears) de Man and Weber pulled the rug out from under them. In fact, however, it is just this kind of abstraction (at the expense of a rigorous, 'contextual' reading of the text) that I am trying to avoid. The abstract problem of unity and division must be reinscribed in the specific textual oppositions between (many different varieties of) separation and merger.

'Structural analysis,' says Jonathan Culler, 'does not move towards a meaning or discover the secret of a text.' And, following Roland Barthes, he says that to read in this way is 'to isolate forms and determine their content and then to treat that content in turn as a form with its own content, to follow, in short, the interplay of surface and envelope.'[22] Whether this would 'satisfy' the ironic skepticism of de Man's argument is hard to say, but it is noteworthy that the problematical, paradoxical opposition of inside and outside, container and content(s), appears in the *Recherche* itself, in the famous, almost prototypical image of the 'carafes' in the Vivonne:

remplies par la rivière où elles sont à leur tour encloses, à la fois
'contenant' aux flancs transparents comme une eau durcie et
'contenu' plongé dans un plus grand contenant de cristal liquide
et courant, évoquaient l'image de la fraîcheur d'une façon plus
délicieuse et plus irritante qu'elles n'eussent fait sur une table
servie, en ne la montrant qu'en fuite dans cette allitération
perpétuelle entre l'eau sans consistance où les mains ne pouvaient
la capter et le verre sans fluidité où le palais ne pourrait en jouir
(I, 168).

Clearly, the physical boundary between water (liquid, flowing
crystal) and glass (solidified water) is transparent but not 'clear,' and
since each is described in terms of the other, the very distinction
between the two is unclear. In short, the division between separation
and merger is itself uncertain, and the two remain alternative but
inseparable possibilities. One could 'analyze' this passage, following
Genette, in the rhetorical terms of metaphor and metonymy,
similarity and contiguity, and one could add, following de Man,
that the inside/outside paradox generates another, more 'personal'
inside/outside paradox since the glass jars in the river are contrasted
with glasses of water standing inside on a dinner table.[23]

And yet the paradoxical water/glass/water image is significant
not only because it is related to numerous other images (metaphors)
of closed jars but because this inside/outside image is itself
'inscribed' in a context of frustrated and ambivalent desire. The
local boys use the carafes to catch fish, but Marcel *cannot* capture the
water with his hands and *cannot* drink the liquid-looking glass: thus
the outdoor 'image' of coolness and refreshment, perpetually 'in
flight' ('flowing,' ironically, like the cool water itself) between the
specific images of water and glass, perpetually beyond his grasp, is
both more delicious and more irritating (more delicious because
more frustrating, more tantalizing) than the familiar indoor image
of water glasses on a table (even though he could not capture that
water or drink that glass either). Marcel's desire to arrest this
perpetual motion, to overcome the barriers that separate him from
the object of his desire, to possess what he cannot possess, is reflected
and 'repeated' in the paradoxical inside/outside, container/con-
tent(s) image of the carafes themselves. This specific inside/outside
image is related, in the larger context of the novel, to the even more
problematical inside/outside dichotomy of self and other, self and

'world.' Indeed, the tripartite water/glass/water image – two zones of glass-like water separated and mediated by a zone of water-like glass – could imply (in this larger context) two alternative and contradictory possibilities: (1) that interior self and exterior world are really the same 'substance' after all, or (2) that the Moebius-strip-like surface of the self is trapped between two alien, enemy zones (interior and exterior), neither of which it can contain or be contained in. Moreover, the desire 'reflected' in the water/glass image, as always in the *Recherche,* is not only the desire to dissolve the barriers and drink the water but also the desire to preserve the barriers (ambiguous and uncertain as they are) and avoid being 'engulfed' by the apparent object of one's desires, engulfed by one's own desires. At the end of this passage Marcel throws some bread into the river, the water suddenly 'solidifies' into egg-shaped clusters of formerly invisible tadpoles, and out of the undifferentiated 'dissolution' of the stream new infant-like creatures are born – an image remarkably similar to the crystallization image at the end of 'Combray I' (pieces of paper dipped into a bowl of water) by which the narrator illustrates the 'flowering' of past memories in (out of) Marcel's cup of tea. Birth itself may be seen as a separation and differentiation from an imagined (watery) unity, but these images of crystallization suggest that it is possible – in a text of implicitly 'metaphorical' signs – to repeat, 'imitate,' and 'reproduce' the process of fertilization and birth so that the tadpoles, flowers, and 'people' born in the river or in the cup of tea remain perpetually suspended there, perpetually new-born, leaving the antithetical desires of merger and separation in a state of perpetual (dis)equilibrium.

It must be added, however, that my emphasis on problematic desires has been anticipated by other critics. Weber himself insists that the 'text in general, and that of Proust in particular, is not the "lieu de sa pensée" but that of his desire'; and his claim that Marcel's desire is 'condemned to oscillate between two equally intolerable poles: the (maternal) absence, which it cannot bear, and the (maternal) presence, which it desires and yet which is its destruction' is precisely what I am trying to show.[24] In fact, both de Man and Weber discuss the literal/allegorical paradoxes of 'Giotto's *Charity,* ' but if de Man concludes that everything in Proust's novel signifies 'something else' (that is, the problem of reading itself), Weber (following Lacan) suggests that this something else is also, in another sense, the 'object of objects,' the fantasized maternal phallus.[25] Here is the crucial difference between formalist (even deconstructive?) readings on the one hand and psychoanalytic readings on the other: for Lacan, a 'structural' psychoanalyst, questions of symbolization and interpretation, rather than being restricted to printed texts, govern all forms of human experience. The linguistic problem of the (differential, relational) sign is also the problem of a subject that finds 'itself' inscribed in the symbolic structures of familial relations and sexual differences. Derrida's practice of turning every philosophical problem into a problem of writing – of discovering 'writing' everywhere, even in Freud's neurological models – might (in theory) lead to the same conclusion, but Derrida's treatment of Freud is rather ambivalent: willing to read Freud's texts, to reconsider the questions Freud raises, he is nonetheless anxious to avoid a 'psychoanalytic' reduction of textual indeterminacy to some original and 'originary' truth.[26] Most 'poststructuralist' critics of literature, even those who claim to be practicing the 'new psychoanalysis' of the French Freudians, retain this ambivalence about the 'application' of Freudian principles to literary criticism. The wish to avoid old-fashioned Freudian reductionism is certainly commendable, but too often these poststructuralist critics, who seem to read all texts as allegories of reading, of the impossibility of reading, read Freud in the same way, so that psychoanalytic theory is merely assimilated to repeated abstract reaffirmations of intellectual paralysis or textual freedom, depending upon how one looks at it.

So, for example, in a recent journal issue devoted to 'Literature and Psychoanalysis,' Shoshana Felman argues that the confrontation of psychoanalysis and literature may be seen as the practice of reading 'otherwise,' against the grain, against any preconceived limitations upon what is a 'true' or 'significant' reading. But she adds that 'literature' is the 'unconscious' of psychoanalysis itself, comprising all possible significations including those that do not 'fit into' conventional Freudian explanations. Rather than applying canonical principles to a fixed text, she would treat the text as a field of open possibilities that can never be delineated in advance – or ever.[27] This sounds promising, a healthy change from Freudian reductionism, but is it a theory at all? Derrida himself contrasts two different kinds of interpretation: 'The one seeks to decipher, dreams of deciphering a truth or an origin which escapes play and the order of the sign, and which lives the necessity of interpretation as an exile.' In contrast to this 'saddened, *negative,* nostalgic, guilty, Rousseauistic' kind of interpretation, the other

> would be the Nietzschean *affirmation,* that is the joyous affirmation of the play of the world and of the innocence of becoming, the affirmation of a world of signs without fault, without truth, and without origin which is offered to an active interpretation.[28]

Of this sort of claim to perpetual self-transcendence, Jonathan Culler comments that it

> invokes quite unashamedly what one might call the myth of the innocence of becoming: that continual change, as an end in itself, is freedom, and that it liberates one from the demands that could be made of any particular state of the system.[29]

In short, there is an ambiguously utopian/nihilistic dimension to poststructuralist thinking, which proclaims either the impossibility of reading or its infinite possibilities.

The resolute assault (by revisionist critics like de Man and Weber) upon the idea that Proust's text is a unified entity is unarguable in its own terms, but it appears to substitute a new, hidden, unifying principle for an old one: not the transcendent unity of art, but the absolute totality of the infinite, contradictory, indeterminable ways of reading the text, which imply no hierarchical order of value and achieve no final truth but are infinite and total nonetheless. The poststructural path leads either to total silence or to the millennium of 'free play.' This may well define the condition of 'the subject,' but, as Fredric Jameson notes:

> In the very act of repudiating any ultimate or transcendental signified, any concept which would dictate the ultimate or fundamental content of reality, Derrida has ended up inventing a new one, namely that of script itself. ... Derrida's own analyses ... depend for their force on the isolation and valoriza-tion of script as a unique and privileged type of content: script has thus become the basic interpretive or explanatory code, one which is felt to have a priority over the other types of content (economic, sexual, and political) which it orders beneath itself in

the hierarchy of the interpretive act . . . [The] choice looks
suspiciously like a metaphysical option, and Derrida's notion of
the trace suspiciously like yet another ontological theory of the
type it was initially designed to denounce.

Jameson may not be right, but as he points out, even in the variety
of 'structuralist' styles – 'whether hermetic or white, whether the
high style and classical pastiche of Lévi-Strauss or the bristling
neologisms of Barthes, whether the self-conscious and over-elaborate
preparatory coquetterie of Lacan or the grim and terroristic
hectoring of Althusser – there is . . . a kind of distance from self.'[30]

Problematics of the 'self' or language about language? Corresponding to the 'poststructuralist' ambivalence about Freud (which
I also share, to a certain extent), I have my own ambivalence about
poststructuralist criticism, particularly the kind that tries to 'appropriate' psychoanalysis for itself. Can Lacan's apparent synthesis of
structuralism and psychoanalysis solve our problems? Weber suggests that the 'object' of Marcel's desires may be seen as the symbolic
object *par excellence,* the (missing) maternal phallus, and Jeffrey
Mehlman, in a Lacanian reading of 'Proust's Counterplot'
– again, the revisionist desire to undermine the overt values and
'truths' of the novel – argues (as does Weber) that the failure of
paternal authority in the episode of the goodnight kiss leaves Marcel
helplessly dependent upon his mother, dependent upon his own
irrational desire to have her all to himself. This fantasized unity of
self and other, child and mother, Lacan calls an 'imaginary' relation,
in contrast to the triangular, structural relationships (mother/
child/father) – mediated by language, by signs, by 'symbolic objects' represented, above all, by the phallus – which he therefore calls
symbolic. The failure of paternal authority is then a failure of
symbolic, structural relations, and (according to Mehlman) Marcel's
desire to become one with his mother represents the same impossible
project as his belief in a language that perfectly represents and
contains 'reality,' in an art that could replace, and be a substitute
for, 'life.'

Mehlman's Lacanian argument has a great deal of validity, but
there are some problems. It is not quite clear why Marcel's desire to
merge with his mother is part of a 'counterplot,' antithetical to the
overt plot of Marcel's aesthetic revelations, if the two are ultimately
identical. And if this counterplot implies an 'underlying logic,'[31] a

secret, unconscious, latent logic opposed to the 'manifest content' of the text, then (rightly or wrongly) it risks falling into the surface/ depth illusion, the attempt to find some deeper truth behind or beneath the false, misleading 'truths' manifested in the text. Indeed, Mehlman seems to imply that Marcel's attitude toward art is a big mistake, that his father *should* have asserted his authority, sent Marcel to bed alone, and forced him to become more self-reliant, in which case he would have escaped being a Mama's boy and avoided all those foolish romantic fantasies about art. But perhaps Mehlman only makes more obvious the moralistic, ideological attitude behind the exchange of a false 'truth' (art) for a true 'nontruth' (the impossibility of art, the infinite possibility of signification). The point is not (I think) simply to challenge Proust's supposed values, to 'disprove' certain attitudes expressed in the text, but to show that the text itself is contradictory, implying multiple, complex, conflict-ing desires which can never be reduced to any single, unified statement of values. Whereas other critics sometimes reduce the text to an overly abstract indeterminacy, Mehlman oversimplifies the conflicts which do not have to be created by anti-idealizing critics since they are inherent in the text itself. His discussion of Marcel's desire to achieve an 'imaginary' (and impossible) unity of mother and son is very much to the point, but he neglects the equally intense desire to maintain divisions and boundaries, to preserve one's autonomy and self-control, to deny one's immediate desires and avoid being overwhelmed by them. The conceptions of memory, time, and even art itself, as they are formulated in Proust's text, reflect not only an original, impossible desire to return to an imaginary unity but a more complex desire (perhaps equally impossible) to keep one's contradictory, conflicting desires in some kind of permanent balance, to pretend to resolve their contradic-tions. One wonders why art, even in Proust's terms, is necessarily an 'imaginary' shortcircuiting of symbolic, structural interrelations.

Both Mehlman and Lacan seem to 'oedipalize' the problem in their identification of symbolic structures with paternal, phallic authority – even if it is a symbolic father rather than an actual one, a symbolic phallus rather than an actual penis. Mehlman calls Marcel an 'Oedipus... at the moment of his incest,'[32] but the fantasized merger of mother and child is not oedipal, not incestuous, not (strictly speaking) sexual. The scene of the goodnight kiss clearly does have an oedipal dimension – underscored by the implicit reference to Abraham's intended sacrifice of Isaac to a higher patriarchal authority – but why is the maternal presence that Marcel wishes so desperately to possess (represented by the kiss itself) necessarily imagined as a *phallus,* as the mother's appropriation of male sexuality? Psychologically, Marcel lives in a preoedipal world, where his father is only an arbitrary, incomprehensible intruder, but this infantile, mother-dominated world, far from being a blissful, womblike union, is a scene of conflict, ambivalence, anxiety, depression, and desperation. Indeed, the various signs that mediate between child and mother,[33] between Marcel and the quasi-maternal, quasi-animistic universe that he is always struggling to incorporate into himself, lest it swallow him up instead – from his mother's kiss to the 'essence' of the hawthorn blossoms to the sudden, unexpected 'impressions' that fill Marcel with joy – *are,* in Lacanian terms, 'symbolic,' signs whose meaning and value depend completely upon other signs, upon the structural relations in which they are 'inscribed.' But they are not necessarily phallic: even the 'fetishistic,' quasi-phallic metaphor of flowers is linked less with older, experienced, 'maternal' women than with adolescent, virginal, tomboyish girls, who resemble adolescent, virginal boys as much as they do the mothers of those boys. In short, as Lacan has shown, fantasies of sexual difference, oedipal structure, and phallic exchange are eminently symbolic,[34] but the primordial sense of absence, loss, and lack (*manque-à-être*) that Lacan represents as the essential problem of the 'subject' is not 'originally' phallic, oedipal, or even sexual. Despite Weber's assertion, the fantasy of a maternal phallus is not the final or original 'symbol' of lost presence but only an oedipal version of a 'deeper,' more fundamental problem.[35]

René Girard's perceptive analysis of 'snobbism' in Proust's novel in terms of 'triangular' or 'mimetic' desire[36] seems, at first glance, to be another kind of oedipal reading: Girard emphasizes the role of rivals, models, and mediators in the dialectic of desire, but as he makes clear in *Violence and the Sacred,* his model is a radical revision (or reversal) of Freud's. For Girard, the Oedipus complex is reduced to a boy's identification with his father, and the boy 'desires' his mother *simply because* he takes his father for a model.[37] An emphasis on ambivalent identification is legitimate and valuable in itself, but Girard seems to believe that life begins at the 'oedipal stage,' that desire means nothing else than sexual relations, that a child's original, infantile dependence on its mother can be ignored, that all children are boys, and that mothers, if they exist at all, are simply an occasion for a boy to wish that he were in his father's shoes. Girard outdoes Freud (and Lacan) in his reduction of psychoanalytic theory to a naively patriarchal model, and one can only say that this incredible misreading of psychoanalysis can be highly illuminating – in the clarity and precision of its argument and in its caricature of Freudian thought. Indeed, the dialectic of (ambivalent) identification and (ambivalent) desire is most relevant, in Proust's novel, to the ('preoedipal') relations of *mother* and son, to the ambiguities of sexual identity, and it is unfortunate that Girard's own analysis of social relations tends to ignore the more directly personal relations of love and jealousy.

As I have already indicated, this account of certain problems in recent Proust criticism is not an attack upon previous work but an attempt to clarify my own 'position,' to show that alternative positions are possible. I have mentioned only those works that seem most influential, most representative of critical problems, or at least most relevant to this study,[38] but the work that I have found most rewarding, most perceptive in its combination of psychological insight and textual analysis, is Leo Bersani's *Marcel Proust: The Fictions of Life and Art,* a book generally neglected by later critics writing from a structuralist or deconstructionist perspective.[39] One need not agree with everything that Bersani says in order to realize that he exposes the conflicts and contradictions in Proust's novel without neglecting its particular textual complexities. My own reading of the *Recherche* parallels Bersani's at several points, but my reading is both more specifically psychoanalytic and more specifically 'contextual' in its attempt to trace the metaphorical/metonymical 'chain of signifiers' in the novel. To cite only one example, my (psychoanalytic) interpretation of the metaphor of flowers – that is, the metaphorical relation between flowers and girls – has no parallel in any previous critical study (including Bersani's).

But as I have been trying to suggest, psychoanalytic interpretation – particularly in the wake of Derrida and Lacan – is not the application of preconceived Freudian formulas, to a literary work, in a tautological attempt to 'discover' an *a priori* 'Freudian' content. On the contrary, it is an attempt to trace the connections between recurrent words or signs in the text, to read each central or marginal 'subtext' in the larger context of the work, and to expose the inconsistencies, contradictions, unanswered questions, and unresolved conflicts which make up the incompletely reconciled 'meanings' of a literary work. It is also an attempt to read each text or subtext in the context of familial relationships and sexual differences, as if each textual sign were 'inscribed' in the differences between men and women, parents and children, self and other. Each signifier in a literary work is inscribed not only in a system of verbal relations *per se* (that of the work, that of the language as a whole) but also in a quasi-linguistic structure of differential 'personal' relationships: and yet this quasi-linguistic structure is itself signified, in any verbal text, by words, by a linguistic chain of signifiers. Instead of trying to fit the text into fixed models of explanation, a psychoanalytic reading of Proust's *Recherche* should force us to confront and reexamine, once again, the kinds of problems that Freudian theory itself addresses.

Notes

Chapter 1: Marcel in Wonderland, or the logic of magical thinking

1   Claude Lévi-Strauss, *Structural Anthropology* (v. 1) (New York: Basic Books, 1963), pp. 167-205. Cf. Dr du Boulbon, the 'alienist' and neurologist in Proust's novel who describes the effect on 'neurotics' (*les nerveux*) of 'cet agent pathogène plus virulent mille fois que tous les microbes, l'idée qu'on est malade' (II, 303). References in the text are to the Pléiade edition of *A la Recherche du temps perdu*, ed. Pierre Clarac and André Ferré, 3 vols (Paris: Gallimard, 1954).
2   See Sigmund Freud, 'Obsessive Actions and Religious Practices,' *The Standard Edition of the Complete Psychological Works of Sigmund Freud*, trans. and ed. James Strachey *et al.*, 24 vols (London: Hogarth Press, 1953-74), vol. 9, pp. 115-27.
3   Cf. Leo Bersani, *Marcel Proust: The Fictions of Life and Art* (New York: Oxford University Press, 1965), pp. 21-55.
4   Cf. Samuel Beckett, *Proust* (New York: Grove Press, 1931), pp. 7-12.
5   See Sigmund Freud, 'Screen Memories,' *Standard Edition*, vol. 3, pp. 305ff, 320-2.
6   Cf. Michel Foucault, *Madness and Civilization* (New York: Random House, 1965), pp. 117-58.
7   For a provocative, zealously psychoanalytic study of the madeleine episode, see Serge Doubrovsky, *La Place de la madeleine* (Paris: Mercure de France, 1974).
8   Cf. Howard Moss, *The Magic Lantern of Marcel Proust* (New York: Macmillan, 1962), pp. 43-62, and Roger Shattuck, *Proust's Binoculars* (New York: Random House, 1963), pp. 3-20, 40-60.
9   See Jacob A. Arlow, 'The Madonna's Conception Through the Eyes,' *Psychoanalytic Study of Society*, no. 3 (1964), pp. 13-25, and also Ernest Jones, 'The Madonna's Conception Through the Ear,' *Essays in Applied Psycho-Analysis* (London: International Psycho-Analytical Press, 1923), pp. 261-359. For a comparable fantasy of the artist as virgin mother, see my discussion of the role of this myth in *Finnegans Wake* in 'The Sane

and Joyful Spirit,' *James Joyce Quarterly*, vol. 13, no. 3 (Spring 1976), pp. 350-65.

10 See Jacob A. Arlow, 'The Madonna's Conception through the Eyes,' *Psychoanalytic Study of Society*, no. 3 (1964), p. 22.

11 Cf. Proust, *Contre Sainte-Beuve* (Paris: Gallimard (Pléiade), 1971), pp. 211-16.

12 Marcel's desire to restore the 'thermodynamic' balance of his overexcited emotions may remind us of Freud's death instinct, in which the pleasurable release of energy tends toward the absolute zero of death. (Cf. Jean Laplanche and J.-B. Pontalis, 'Death Instincts,' *The Language of Psychoanalysis* (New York: Norton, 1974), pp. 97-103, and Jean Laplanche, *Life and Death in Psychoanalysis* (Baltimore: The Johns Hopkins University Press, 1976), pp. 103-24.) However, his longing for an almost deathlike tranquillity is *not* an inborn instinct but, essentially, an obsessional strategy – born out of guilt and anxiety – for greater self-control and self-sufficiency.

13 Cf. Weston La Barre's excellent study *The Ghost Dance: Origins of Religion* (Garden City: Doubleday, 1970).

14 See Claude Lévi-Strauss, *The Savage Mind* (University of Chicago Press, 1966).

Chapter 2: The 'economic' problem in Proust and Freud

1 Proust, *Correspondance avec sa mère*, ed. Philip Kolb (Paris: Plon, 1953), p. 97.

2 See Alison Winton, 'The Developing Role of Money in Proust's *A la Recherche du temps perdu*,' *French Studies*, vol. 31, no. 2 (April 1977), pp. 164-81.

3 In fact, Proust himself donated his *mother's* furniture, after her death, to the original of Jupien's homosexual brothel. See George D. Painter, *Proust: The Later Years* (Boston: Little, Brown, 1965), p. 267.

4 The little pavilion resembles an old toll-house (I, 492).

5 See Chapter 4 of this study.

6 Serge Doubrovsky, who links the *petit pavillon* with the *cabinet* at Combray and with the episode of the madeleine, is one of the few critics to pay much attention to this scene. See *La Place de la madeleine* (Paris: Mercure de France, 1974).

7 Samuel Beckett, *Three Novels* (New York: Grove Press, 1965), p. 383.

8 See Sigmund Freud, 'Character and Anal Erotism' and 'On Transformations of Instinct as Exemplified in Anal Erotism,' *Standard Edition*, vol. 9, pp. 169-75, and vol. 17, pp. 127-33, and Norman O. Brown, *Life Against Death* (New York: Vintage Books, 1959), pp. 234-304.

9 See the entries for 'Economic,' 'Pleasure Principle,' 'Principle of

Constancy,' and 'Death Instincts' in Jean Laplanche and J.-B. Pontalis, *The Language of Psychoanalysis* (New York: Norton, 1974). See also Laplanche, *Life and Death in Psychoanalysis* (Baltimore: The Johns Hopkins University Press, 1976), and Paul Ricoeur, *Freud and Philosophy* (New Haven: Yale University Press, 1970).

10 See 'Ego-Libido/Object-Libido,' *The Language of Psychoanalysis*, pp. 150-1, and Sigmund Freud, 'On Narcissism: An Introduction,' *Standard Edition*, vol. 14, pp. 73-102.

11 See, for example, Jacques Derrida, 'Structure, Sign, and Play in the Discourse of the Human Sciences,' *Writing and Difference*, trans. Alan Bass (University of Chicago Press, and London: Routledge & Kegan Paul, 1978), pp. 278-93, and *Of Grammatology*, trans. Gayatri Chakravorty Spivak (Baltimore: The Johns Hopkins University Press, 1976).

12 For recent psychoanalytic criticism of Freud's metapsychological theory of drive and energy, see, for example, George S. Klein, *Psychoanalytic Theory* (New York: International Universities Press, 1976), esp. pp. 41-120; Merton M. Gill and Philip S. Holzman (eds), *Psychology versus Metapsychology, Psychological Issues*, vol. 9, no. 4, Monograph 36 (New York: International Universities Press, 1976); Roy Schafer, *A New Language for Psychoanalysis* (New Haven: Yale University Press, 1976); and Louis Breger, 'Psychoanalysis Is *Not* Science,' *Freud's Unfinished Journey: Conventional and Critical Perspectives in Psychoanalytic Theory* (London and Boston: Routledge & Kegan Paul, 1981).

13 Paul Ricoeur, *Freud and Philosophy* (New Haven: Yale University Press, 1970), and Jacques Derrida, 'Freud and the Scene of Writing,' *Writing and Difference*, pp. 196-231.

14 Jacques Derrida, 'La parole soufflée,' *Writing and Difference*, p. 175.

15 For this kind of interpretation down to the *letter*, see Roland Barthes, *S/Z* (New York: Hill & Wang, 1974), pp. 106-7, and (less convincingly) Serge Doubrovsky, *La Place de la madeleine*.

16 See Jacques Derrida, 'From Restricted to General Economy: A Hegelianism without Reserve,' *Writing and Difference*, pp. 251-77, and 'La Pharmacie de Platon,' *La Dissémination* (Paris: Seuil, 1972), pp. 69-197.

17 Cf. Jacques Derrida, 'White Mythology: Metaphor in the Text of Philosophy,' *New Literary History*, vol. 6, no. 1 (Autumn 1974), pp. 5-74.

18 Sigmund Freud, 'Psychoanalytic Notes Upon an Autobiographical Account of a Case of Paranoia,' *Standard Edition*, vol. 12, pp. 78-9.

19 On the 'exchange-value' of money and words, see Michel Foucault, *The Order of Things* (New York: Vintage, 1973), pp. 166-214, and also Marc Shell, *The Economy of Literature* (Baltimore: The Johns Hopkins University Press, 1978).

Chapter 3: Bonds of love and kinship

1 Cf. Jeffrey Mehlman, *A Structural Study of Autobiography* (Ithaca: Cornell University Press, 1974), pp. 33-5.

2 See George D. Painter, *Proust: The Later Years* (Boston: Little, Brown, 1965), p. 268.

3 On sadism and masochism see Jean Laplanche, *Life and Death in Psychoanalysis* (Baltimore: The Johns Hopkins University Press, 1976); Leo Bersani, *Baudelaire and Freud* (Berkeley: University of California Press, 1977), pp. 75-89; Gilles Deleuze, *Masochism* (New York: Braziller, 1971), although Deleuze disputes the idea that sadism and masochism may be complementary aspects of a single personality; and Robert J. Stoller, *Perversion: The Erotic Form of Hatred* (New York: Dell, 1975).

4 Sigmund Freud, 'A Child Is Being Beaten,' *Standard Edition,* vol. 17, pp. 177-203.

5 Sigmund Freud, 'Mourning and Melancholia,' *Standard Edition,* vol. 14, pp. 243-58.

6 Cf. Gregory Zilboorg, 'The Discovery of the Oedipus Complex,' *Psychoanalytic Quarterly,* no. XIII (1939), pp. 279-302.

7 See Sigmund Freud, 'Family Romances,' *Standard Edition,* vol. 9, pp. 237-41.

8 See Sigmund Freud, 'A Special Type of Choice of Object Made by Men' and 'On the Universal Tendency to Debasement in the Sphere of Love,' *Standard Edition,* vol. 11, pp. 165-90.

9 See Bruno Bettelheim, *Symbolic Wounds* (New York: Collier Books, 1962); Philip Slater, *The Glory of Hera* (Boston: Beacon Press, 1968); and Robert J. Stoller, *Perversion: The Erotic Form of Hatred* (New York: Dell, 1975), pp. 135-62.

10 See Justin O'Brien, 'Albertine the Ambiguous,' *PMLA,* no. 64 (December 1949), pp. 933-52, and Harry Levin, 'Proust, Gide, and the Sexes,' *PMLA,* no. 65 (June 1950), pp. 648-52.

11 Cf. Leo Bersani's excellent discussion of 'The Anguish and Inspiration of Jealousy' in *Marcel Proust: The Fictions of Life and Art* (New York: Oxford University Press, 1965), pp. 56-97, and also René Girard's analysis of 'triangular' desire in *Deceit, Desire, and the Novel* (Baltimore: The Johns Hopkins University Press, 1965).

12 Cf. Jacques Lacan, 'Seminar on "The Purloined Letter,"' *French Freud, Yale French Studies,* no. 48 (1972), pp. 39-72.

13 Marcel Mauss, *The Gift (*New York: Norton, 1967).

14 Cf. Claude Lévi-Strauss, *The Elementary Structures of Kinship* (Boston: Beacon Press, 1969).

15 On the relation of Proust's novel to the (social) realist tradition, see Richard Terdiman's fine study *The Dialectics of Isolation: Self and Society*

in the French Novel from the Realists to Proust (New Haven: Yale University Press, 1976).

Chapter 4: Proust, Joyce, and the metaphor of flowers

1 Marcel associates the pink flowers with certain special foods, but I don't think this 'oral' interest exhausts the reasons for his fascination with them. For a detailed stylistic analysis of the hawthorn passages, see Jean Milly, *La Phrase de Proust* (Paris: Larousse, 1975), pp. 97-131.

2 See Sigmund Freud, 'Fetishism,' *Standard Edition*, vol. 21, pp. 152-7. See also 'The Taboo of Virginity,' *Standard Edition*, vol. 11, pp. 193-208.

3 References to Joyce's writings, in the text, are from the following editions: *A Portrait of the Artist as a Young Man* (New York: Viking Press, 1964), *Stephen Hero* (New York: New Directions, 1963), *Ulysses* (New York: Vintage, 1961), and *Finnegans Wake* (New York: Viking Press, 1959). In the text these works are referred to as P, SH, U and FW respectively.

4 See Mark Shechner, *Joyce in Nighttown* (Berkeley: University of California Press, 1974), pp. 211-19.

5 See Bruno Bettelheim, *Symbolic Wounds* (New York: Collier Books, 1962).

6 Cf. Ernest Jones, 'The Symbolic Significance of Salt in Folklore and Superstition,' *Essays in Applied Psycho-Analysis* (London: International Psycho-Analytical Press, 1923), pp. 112-203.

7 See Sigmund Freud, 'On the Sexual Theories of Children,' *Standard Edition*, vol. 9, pp. 205-26.

8 Samuel Beckett, 'Dante, Bruno, Vico, Joyce,' in *Our Exagmination Round His Factification For Incamination of Work in Progress* (Norfolk, Conn.: New Directions, 1939), p. 14.

9 See Jacques Derrida, *Of Grammatology* (Baltimore: The Johns Hopkins University Press, 1976).

10 Ernest Jones, 'The Madonna's Conception Through the Ear,' *Essays in Applied Psycho-Analysis* (London: International Pyscho-Analytical Press, 1923), pp. 261-359. See also my article, 'The Sane and Joyful Spirit,' *James Joyce Quarterly*, vol. 13, no. 3 (Spring 1976), pp. 350-65.

11 See Jacob A. Arlow, 'The Madonna's Conception Through the Eyes,' *Psychoanalytic Study of Society*, no. 3 (1964), pp. 13-25.

12 Cf. Gilles Deleuze, *Proust and Signs* (New York: Braziller, 1972).

13 Jacques Lacan, 'The Agency of the Letter in the Unconscious,' *Ecrits: A Selection*, trans. Alan Sheridan (New York: Norton, 1977), pp. 146-78. See also Jean Laplanche and Serge Leclaire, 'The Unconscious: A Psychoanalytic Study,' *French Freud, Yale French Studies*, no. 48 (1972),

pp. 118-75, and Anika Lemaire, *Jacques Lacan,* trans. David Macey (London: Routledge & Kegan Paul, 1977).

14 On the 'symbolism' of flowers in dreams, including red flowers, see Sigmund Freud, 'The Interpretation of Dreams,' *Standard Edition,* vol. 4, p. 319, and vol. 5, pp. 347-8, 374-6. Cf. the ambiguous identification of flowers with male homosexuals in Jean Genet's *Notre Dame des Fleurs* and the identification of red poppies with bloody wounds in two poems by Sylvia Plath, 'Poppies in October' and 'Poppies in July,' *Ariel* (New York: Harper & Row, 1966), pp. 19, 81. Cf. also Robert Rogers, *Metaphor: A Psychoanalytic View* (Berkeley: University of California Press, 1978), pp. 113-30.

15 Claude Lévi-Strauss, 'The Structural Study of Myth,' *Structural Anthropology* (v. 1) (New York: Basic Books, 1963), p. 229.

16 See Jacques Derrida, 'White Mythology: Metaphor in the Text of Philosophy'; 'Differance,' included with *Speech and Phenomena* (Evanston: Northwestern University Press, 1973), pp. 129-60; and 'La Pharmacie de Platon,' *La Dissémination* (Paris: Seuil, 1972), pp. 69-197.

17 Cf. Jacques Lacan, 'The Signification of the Phallus,' *Ecrits: A Selection,* pp. 281-91.

Chapter 5: Reminiscence, metaphor, and art

1 See Sigmund Freud, *Beyond the Pleasure Principle, Standard Edition,* vol. 18, pp. 14-17.

2 Cf. Jacques Lacan, 'The Mirror Stage as Formative of the Function of the I,' *Ecrits: A Selection* (New York: Norton, 1977), pp. 1-7.

3 See George S. Klein, *Psychoanalytic Theory* (New York: International Universities Press, 1976), pp. 259-79.

4 Sigmund Freud, 'The "Uncanny,"' *Standard Edition,* vol. 17, pp. 217-51.

5 See Serge Doubrovsky, *La Place de la madeleine* (Paris: Mercure de France, 1974).

6 Cf. Roger Shattuck, *Marcel Proust* (New York: Viking, 1974), p. 86.

7 Proust, 'A propos du "style" de Flaubert,' in *Contre Sainte-Beuve* (Paris: Gallimard (Pléiade), 1971), pp. 586-600.

8 On the central Proustian problem of the interpretation and translation of signs – especially the structure of reminiscences and its relation to language – see the works by Gilles Deleuze, Gérard Genette, Georges Poulet, Paul de Man, and Samuel Weber cited in the notes to Chapter 7. On the significance of metaphor and metonymy generally, see Roman Jakobson, 'Two Aspects of Language and Two Types of Aphasic Disturbances,' *Selected Writings II* (The Hague: Mouton, 1971), pp. 239-59; Roland Barthes, *Elements of Semiology* (New York: Hill & Wang, 1968), pp. 58-60; David Lodge, *The Modes of Modern Writing: Metaphor, Metonymy, and the Typology of Modern Literature* (Ithaca: Cornell

University Press, 1977); as well as Jacques Derrida, 'White Mythology: Metaphor in the Text of Philosophy,' *New Literary History,* vol. 6, no. 1 (Autumn 1974), pp. 5-74. See also Jacques Lacan, 'The Agency of the Letter in the Unconscious,' *Ecrits: A Selection* (New York: Norton, 1977); and Jean Laplanche and Serge Leclaire, 'The Unconscious: A Psychoanalytic Study,' *French Freud, Yale French Studies,* no. 48 (1972), pp. 118-75.

9 Cf. Proust, *Contre Sainte-Beuve* (Paris: Gallimard (Pléiade), 1971), p. 216.
10 Cf. the works of Gilles Deleuze, Paul de Man, Samuel Weber and Jacques Derrida already referred to and the notion of the 'scriptible' in Barthes, *S/Z* (New York: Hill & Wang, 1974).
11 Proust, 'A propos du "style" de Flaubert,' in *Contre Sainte-Beuve* (Paris: Gallimard (Pléiade), 1971), p. 586.

Chapter 6: Proust's myth of artistic creation

1 See esp. Thomas Weiskel's excellent study *The Romantic Sublime* (Baltimore: The Johns Hopkins University Press, 1976).
2 See Weston La Barre, *The Ghost Dance: Origins of Religion* (Garden City: Doubleday, 1970), pp. 357-82.
3 It may be significant that Marcel's reminiscence of his grandmother at Balbec is a memory of her helping him off with his boots (II, 755-7).
4 Cf. George S. Klein, *Psychoanalytic Theory* (New York: International Universities Press, 1976), pp. 259-79.
5 D. H. Lawrence, *Sons and Lovers* (New York: Viking, 1958), pp. 410, 420, 354, 287-88, 287.
6 D. H. Lawrence, *Women in Love* (Harmondsworth: Penguin, 1976), pp. 193, 191, 192, 192, 178, 186.
7 For a largely empirical study of early mother-child relations, see John Bowlby, *Attachment and Loss* (v. 1, *Attachment;* v. 2, *Separation*) (New York: Basic Books, 1969 and 1973).
8 See Mark Poster's excellent study *Critical Theory of the Family* (New York: The Seabury Press, 1978).
9 Jacques Lacan's notions of 'castration' and of the symbolism of the phallus (as indicated, for example, in 'The Signification of the Phallus') are subtle and complex, but they remain disturbingly 'phallocentric.' See Chapter 7.
10 See Sigmund Freud, 'On the Sexual Theories of Children,' *Standard Edition,* vol. 9, pp. 205-26, and Bruno Bettelheim, *Symbolic Wounds* (New York: Collier Books, 1962).
11 On the question of sexual identity, see Robert J. Stoller, *Perversion: The Erotic Form of Hatred* (New York: Dell, 1975), pp. 135-62; Robert J. Stoller, *Sex and Gender,* 2 vols (New York: Jason Aronson, 1968 and 1975); and Nancy Chodorow's indispensable study *The Reproduction of*

Mothering: Psychoanalysis and the Sociology of Gender (Berkeley: University of California Press, 1978).

12 Euripides, *The Bacchae and Other Plays,* trans. Philip Vellacott (Harmondsworth: Penguin, 1954).

13 On the sexual ambiguity of shamans, see Weston La Barre, *The Ghost Dance: Origins of Religion* (Garden City: Doubleday, 1970), pp. 315-16. Cf. Bruno Bettelheim, *Symbolic Wounds,* pp. 111-13.

14 Cf. Philip Slater, *The Glory of Hera* (Boston: Beacon Press, 1968), esp, pp. 292-301.

15 Cf. Sigmund Freud, 'Mourning and Melancholia,' *Standard Edition,* vol. 14, pp. 243-58; and John Bowlby, *Separation.*

Chapter 7: Theoretical conclusion: psychoanalysis, literary theory, and recent Proust criticism

1 See esp. Jacques Lacan, 'The Agency of the Letter in the Unconscious or Reason Since Freud,' *Ecrits: A Selection* (New York: Norton, 1977). See also Anthony Wilden, 'Lacan and the Discourse of the Other,' in *The Language of the Self* (New York: Delta, 1968), pp. 159-311, and Anika Lemaire, *Jacques Lacan* (London: Routledge & Kegan Paul, 1977).

2 See Paul Ricoeur, *Freud and Philosophy* (New Haven: Yale University Press, 1970), p. 32.

3 Sigmund Freud, *The Interpretation of Dreams, Standard Edition,* vol. 5, pp. 350-3. Cf. also Paul Ricoeur, *Freud and Philosophy* and Charles Rycroft, 'Symbolism and its Relationship to the Primary and Secondary Processes' and 'Beyond the Reality Principle,' *Imagination and Reality* (New York: International Universities Press, 1968), pp. 42-60, 102-13.

4 Michael Sherwood, *The Logic of Explanation in Psychoanalysis* (New York: Academic Press, 1969).

5 Cf. Jean Laplanche and J. B. Pontalis, 'Fantasy and the Origins of Sexuality,' *International Journal of Psycho-Analysis,* no. 49 (1968), pp. 1-18. ('Fantasme originaire, fantasmes des origines, origine du fantasme,' *Les Temps modernes,* no. 19 (1964), pp. 1833-68.)

6 Calling the *Recherche* a novel seems, in itself, to be a critical judgment, implying a continuity between Proust's text and conventionally 'realistic' novels of the nineteenth century, but I am making no such judgment and, as Fredric Jameson suggests, the form of the novel may be so changeable that 'each one is different, a leap in the void, an invention of content simultaneous with the invention of the form' *(The Prison-House of Language* (Princeton University Press, 1972), p. 73).

7 Jeffrey Mehlman, *A Structural Study of Autobiography* (Ithaca: Cornell

University Press, 1974), p. 63. The quotation from Sollers is from 'Le Monde au téléscope,' *Le Nouvel observateur,* 11 July 1971, p. 41.

8 Georges Poulet, *Proustian Space* (Baltimore: The Johns Hopkins University Press, 1977 (1963)), pp. 79ff.

9 Ibid., p. 101. See also Samuel M. Weber, 'The Madrepore,' *MLN,* vol. 87, no. 7 (December 1972), pp. 921-2.

10 Gilles Deleuze, *Proust and Signs* (New York: Braziller, 1972), pp. 90, 40-1, 149.

11 Gérard Genette, 'Proust palimpseste,' *Figures* (Paris: Seuil, 1966), pp. 39-67; 'Proust et le langage indirect,' *Figures II* (Paris: Seuil, 1969), pp. 223-94; 'Métonymie chez Proust,' *Figures III* (Paris: Seuil, 1972), pp. 41-63. In 'Discours du récit' (in *Figures III*) Genette uses Proust's text to analyze narrative forms and structures, but these formal classifications are not immediately relevant here.

12 *Figures II,* p. 293.

13 *Figures III,* p. 63.

14 Paul de Man, 'Semiology and Rhetoric,' *Diacritics* (Fall 1973), p. 28.

15 Samuel M. Weber, 'The Madrepore,' pp. 926-7.

16 Ibid., p. 918.

17 Paul de Man, 'Proust et l'allégorie de la lecture,' in *Mouvements premiers: études critiques offertes à Georges Poulet* (Paris: Corti, 1971), p. 250. In slightly different form, the two essays of de Man cited here now form part of his recent book *Allegories of Reading* (New Haven: Yale University Press, 1979), pp. 3-19, 57-78.

18 Paul de Man, 'Semiology and Rhetoric,' pp. 27-8.

19 Samuel M. Weber, 'The Madrepore,' p. 918.

20 See Roman Jakobson, 'Two Aspects of Language and Two Types of Aphasic Disturbances,' *Selected Writings II* (The Hague: Mouton, 1977), pp. 239-59; and also David Lodge, *The Modes of Modern Writing: Metaphor, Metonymy, and the Typology of Modern Literature* (Ithaca: Cornell University Press, 1977), pp. 73-124.

21 Jonathan Culler, 'Commentary,' *New Literary History,* vol. 6, no. 1 (Autumn 1974), p. 229.

22 Jonathan Culler, *Structuralist Poetics* (Ithaca: Cornell University Press, 1975, and London: Routledge & Kegan Paul, 1974), p. 259.

23 See Gérard Genette, *Figures III,* p. 54; Paul de Man, 'Proust et l'allégorie de la lecture,' pp. 233ff., and 'Semiology and Rhetoric,' p. 31; and also Gilles Deleuze, *Proust and Signs,* pp. 104ff.

24 Samuel M. Weber, 'The Madrepore,' pp. 927, 944. In the second passage, does Weber really mean that Marcel's desire desires (presence)?

25 Ibid., p. 948. (Note that Weber identifies a comparison to a *cuisinière* in the description of Giotto's *Charity* with the *fille de cuisine* (that is, 'Giotto's Charity') while de Man identifies this same comparison with the actual 'cook' Françoise.) More on the 'maternal phallus' later.

26 On the oddly literal 'Freudian symbolism' in Jacques Derrida, note Fredric Jameson, pp. 178-9.

27 Shoshana Felman, ' To Open the Question' and 'Turning the Screw of Interpretation.' *Yale French Studies,* nos 55/56 (1977), pp. 5-10, 94-207.

28 Jacques Derrida, *Writing and Difference* (University of Chicago Press, and London, Routledge & Kegan Paul, 1978), p. 292.

29 Jonathan Culler, *Structuralist Poetics,* p. 251.

30 Fredric Jameson, pp. 182-3, 209.

31 Jeffrey Mehlman, p. 63.

32 Ibid., p. 25.

33 Cf. D. W. Winnicott, 'Transitional Objects and Transitional Phenomena,' *Through Paediatrics to Psycho-Analysis* (New York: Basic Books, 1975), pp. 229-42.

34 See Jacques Lacan, 'The Signification of the Phallus,' *Ecrits: A Selection,* pp. 281-91. Cf. Anthony Wilden, 'Lacan and the Discourse of the Other,' pp. 186-8; Anika Lemaire, *Jacques Lacan,* pp. 82-8; and (on Lacan's 'phallogocentrism') Jacques Derrida, 'The Purveyor of Truth,' *Yale French Studies,* no. 52 (1975), pp. 31-113.

35 See Robert J. Stoller, *Perversion: The Erotic Form of Hatred* (New York: Dell, 1975), and *Sex and Gender,* 2 vols (New York: Jason Aronson, 1968 and 1975); and Nancy Chodorow, *The Reproduction of Mothering: Psychoanalysis and the Sociology of Gender* (Berkeley: University of California Press, 1978).

36 René Girard, *Deceit, Desire, and the Novel* (Baltimore: The Johns Hopkins University Press, 1965 (1961)).

37 René Girard, *Violence and the Sacred* (Baltimore: The Johns Hopkins University Press, 1977 (1972)), esp. pp. 169-92.

38 Of many other valuable studies, I would like to mention these psychoanalytic studies of Proust's work: Gregory Zilboorg, 'The Discovery of the Oedipus Complex,' *Psychoanalytic Quarterly,* no. XIII (1939), pp. 279-302; Milton Miller, *Nostalgia: A Psychoanalytic Study of Marcel Proust* (Boston: Houghton Mifflin, 1956); more recently, Ghislaine Florival, *Le Désir chez Proust* (Paris: Nauwelaerts, 1971); and esp. Serge Doubrovsky's fruitful and provocative *La Place de la madeleine* (Paris: Mercure de France, 1974).

39 Leo Bersani's later work has become more theoretical, psychoanalytic, and (in part) Lacanian: see *A Future for Astyanax* (Boston: Little, Brown, 1976) and *Baudelaire and Freud* (Berkeley: University of California Press, 1977).

Index